...rn in 1962, Colin Fry received his first message at the a... of four and became a working medium at seventeen. ... tours internationally and is the acclaimed star of ... television shows *6ixth Sense, Psychic Private Eyes* and ...*in Fry Live*, and has now reached a worldwide audience ...6 million regular viewers. One of the top mediums in ...e psychic mediumship community, Colin uses his ...al knowledge to offer life-changing advice and ...ort to people, providing sensible down-to-earth ...nations about the unusual world of the para-...nal and supernatural. He is the bestselling author of ...*efore Death, Secrets of the Afterlife* and *The Message*.

The Happy Medium

My Psychic Life

Colin Fry

LONDON · SYDNEY · AUCKLAND · JOHANNESBURG

1 3 5 7 9 10 8 6 4 2

First published in Great Britain in 2012 by Rider,
an imprint of Ebury Publishing
A Random House Group Company

The Random House Group Limited Reg. No. 954009

Addresses for companies within the Random House Group can be found at:
www.randomhouse.co.uk

A CIP catalogue record for this book is available from the British Library

The Forest Stewardship Council Limited supports The Forest Stewardship
Council [FSC], the leading international forest certification organisation.
Our books carrying the FSC label are printed on FSC® certified paper.
FSC® is the only forest certification scheme endorsed by the leading
environmental organisations, including Greenpeace. Our paper procurement
policy can be found at www.randomhouse.co.uk/environment

Printed and bound by CPI Group (UK) Ltd, Croydon, CR0 4YY

ISBN 9781846043406

Copies are available at special rates for bulk orders. Contact the sales
development team on 020 7840 8487 for more information

To buy books by your favourite authors and register for offers visit:
www.randomhouse.co.uk

I dedicate this book to my family and friends, to my civil partner Mikey, to everyone who has been a part of my life.

To Tony Lewis and Kevin Elliott, Jenny and Sean (who keep me sane!) and to David and Julia, who have kept me going when I've wanted to give up.

To Paul (Vince) and Chris who've been such a big part of the story so far – glad we all survived it!

With my love and affection,
Colin

Contents

Foreword

I WAS seventeen years old when a fellow medium told me that I would one day write my life story. I laughed at her at the time. I had barely left school and had only just got my first job. I thought it was nonsense. 'Who on earth would want to read that?' I said to myself. But here I am, more than three decades later, having finally put my story down on paper.

If the idea that I would write my autobiography seemed far-fetched thirty years ago, the notion that I might call it *The Happy Medium* would have felt even more ridiculous. The truth was that for much of my early life I was far from happy; quite the opposite. I endured a lot of pain, so much so that I once contemplated ending it all.

Today I understand that unhappiness and suffering are as important a part of life as joy and happiness. Indeed, for a medium it is essential to experience the dark as well as the light in life.

This was something else I was told when I was a young, developing medium. 'You have to have some grey hairs,' was how my mentor at the time put it to me, rather wisely. But again, I didn't understand it at the time. Now that I have turned fifty, and have quite a few well concealed grey hairs, I understand that she was absolutely right.

I now know that to be a successful medium, you have to go through hardship in life. Because you are so intensely involved in communicating and interpreting the feelings and emotions and memories of other people, you have to have experienced those highs and lows yourself. It's what makes the difference between a good medium and a not-so-good one.

And so this book is not just the story of the personal highs and lows of my life. It is the story of how I became a happy person – and a happy medium too. I hope you enjoy it.

COLIN FRY

1 | 'Not Long'

IN the three decades since I first began practising as a medium I have received communications from many thousands of spirits who have crossed over to the other side.

These messages come in different forms – from individuals from all walks of life, from all colours and creeds, and from all corners of the world. In the vast majority of cases, I encounter these spirits only once. Invariably, they have a message they need to pass on to a loved one who is with me, either at a demonstration or a personal reading. Once that has been achieved, they are at peace and move on.

A small handful of spirits have contacted me on more than one occasion, however. And an even smaller number have been doing so throughout my psychic life, ever since I first began to communicate with the spirit world as a young boy. One of these is the spirit of a young woman. Her presence is a very ephemeral one. I have no clairvoyant vision of her; in other words, she doesn't appear in front of me, as some spirits do. So I don't know what she looks like.

But I have felt her presence from her voice and the energy, and I have become convinced that she is in her early thirties and is the mother of many children. She is also, in the literal sense of the phrase, a troubled soul.

I first heard her voice as a boy of ten. Since the very beginning, her communications have always been brief; indeed, they always consist of just the same two words: 'Not long.' However, I have learned to take these two words very seriously indeed whenever I hear them. They always indicate that someone who is physically close to me at the time will soon be passing over. Now, some people might regard this as slightly unsettling, as an ominous and frightening thing. But I have to say that, as a medium, this has actually been a great comfort to me, because it has allowed me to prepare for people's death. I heard this woman's voice shortly before the passing of both my grandfathers and grandmothers. She has also come before the loss of three close friends. She has helped me enormously.

As I say, I first heard her voice when I was a schoolboy but it is only recently that I have learned who she is and truly understood her significance in my story. I now firmly believe the voice is that of my great-grandmother, a lady called Minnie Carter. My story must begin with her story because the two – along with the story of her daughter, my grandmother – are inextricably linked.

*

The precise details of Minnie Carter's life are shrouded in mystery and it's only been in recent years that I, my mother and brother have begun to piece together her story. It is a fascinating – and tragic – one, nevertheless.

Minnie was probably married to a man named George Smith. I say 'probably' because it's not certain that they were ever officially man and wife. They must have been quite an unusual couple in those very strait-laced times. Smith wasn't even my great-grandfather's real name. We think George was in fact Jewish and had come to England from Poland with his father to escape persecution there. There's some evidence that he and Minnie lived in Kent but then ended up in London, where they had nine children together. One of the youngest of them, Lilian, born around 1903, was my grandmother.

It seems that Minnie had a connection to the world of mediumship and the paranormal. According to a great-aunt, who had known her and spoke about her to a relative, Minnie had come from gypsy stock and had once been arrested and prosecuted under the Witchcraft and Vagrancy Act. It's not quite clear what she had done. In the nineteenth century, you could be prosecuted for a variety of offences, from conducting psychic readings to looking at a set of tarot cards. She may have simply been reading tea leaves. Whatever her offence was, the punishment was severe.

The great-aunt recalled that the courts fined my great-grandmother fourteen shillings, which she couldn't pay. So Minnie was put in the London assizes (where they also had cells for short-term convictions) for fourteen days and had to take two of her younger children with her. Now, it was said that my grandmother was one of them, but when you work out the dates it couldn't have been. It must have been two of the older children.

How Minnie's incarceration affected her relationship with George is unclear, although the fact that he didn't offer to release her from her imprisonment doesn't reflect well on him. According to the great-aunt, their relationship was fractious. It must have been, because it came to an end one terrible day when my great-grandmother was thirty-two years of age. That evening my great-grandfather arrived home cradling a ginger-haired young baby, a boy called Frederick. George calmly announced that he was his child by another woman and that Minnie must bring him up as her own.

I can't even begin to imagine how devastating this must have been, but it was clearly too much for my great-grandmother to bear. Minnie's response was to commit suicide by drinking glass filings that she'd put in a glass of milk. It must have been an agonising, awful death. And as well as robbing them of their mother, it had the most appalling impact on Minnie's children, and my grandmother in particular.

In the wake of Minnie's passing, all nine of the children – including the baby, Frederick – were split up and sent to live in different places. They were effectively thrown to the four winds and into the hands of public charity. My grandmother, who was a three-year-old at the time, was shipped off to a Roman Catholic orphanage where she was raised by nuns. Her sister Vi was sent by Barnardo's to Canada. The rest were distributed to other orphanages, charities and refuges.

It sounds unbelievable but my great-grandfather simply turned his back on all of his children with Minnie. He moved to Epping Forest where he proceeded to marry his housekeeper and have two more daughters. He had nothing to do with his children at all until many, many years later. To be honest, it was amazing that they ever felt able to see him. I'm not sure I could have forgiven him for what he did.

My grandmother's childhood was solitary and very harsh. It wasn't until she was about fifteen that she even realised that she had brothers and sisters. By that time her life had become even more miserable, if that was possible.

At around the age of fourteen she was put into service and was sent to live with this incredibly cruel family who beat her. When she – understandably – ran away, the police were informed, who arrested her and dragged her back to the house, where she was duly chained to a mangle that was guarded by a bulldog.

Even Dickens couldn't have imagined anything quite so brutal.

When she ran away for a second time, the authorities decided that she must be insane to keep running away from this respectable family. She was put into an asylum at the age of fifteen. She might have remained there for the rest of her life if it hadn't been for her long lost brothers.

By this time, in the wake of the end of World War I, the two oldest brothers, Charles and Will, were trying to retrace the family. Being that little bit older, they remembered the family before it had been broken up and wanted to put it back together again. They had both served in the trenches, where Will got hit by mustard gas, as a result of which he suffered bronchial problems for the rest of his life. Charles fared a little better, however, and was something of a show business success story. He was a gifted musician, a trumpet player, and joined the Army Band before becoming a member of a band led by the famous Henry Hall and also of the Bournemouth Symphony Orchestra.

Anyhow, Charles and Will had begun tracing the family and had successfully found all their brothers and sisters, including Vi in Canada. My grandmother was the last one that they found. To their horror, they discovered that Lilian had been sent to this institution for no real reason – something that happened a lot in those days. They made an application to have her released, which was denied. So Will and Charles decided to take the law into their own hands. Late one night they got a horse and cart, broke into the home and my grandmother's cell – then stole her away. She was taken to my great-great-aunt in Havant, where she hid for a couple of weeks until the authorities gave up their search for her. She was then moved to Hove, where she lived a quiet life with Will and his wife Daisy.

It was almost as if my grandmother had started her life all over again. She went to work as a maid for a respectable gentlemen's club in Brighton. There she met my grandfather Lawrie – Laurence Briggs – who was a bellboy. They were both in their late thirties and found love late in life, particularly for that time. She was in her late thirties when she had my mother, Margaret, in 1940.

Of Minnie Carter's nine children, it seems that only one of them inherited her unusual gifts: my grandmother. In years to come, Lilian would also play a significant part in my psychic development.

My father's side of the family didn't have quite as dramatic a background as my mother's, although they had their moments. My paternal grandmother was a lady named Freda Hutchins. She was very proud of her Scottish heritage, something that I have maintained. Through her I am entitled to wear the McDonald tartan, which I do occasionally.

My paternal grandfather was Douglas Fry. When my grandmother and he first met, he was a mechanic, but also a very skilled pianist. Sadly music was a dream of his that was never fulfilled. His disappointment at being denied the opportunity to make use of his skill had very sad consequences in the way that he treated his children – in particular, my father and his talents.

It's fair to say that Douglas was a strange man. He would swing from being the life and soul of the party, funny and witty, to being quite a scary man. He was a man with whom I had a challenging relationship when I was a child. He could be verbally volatile and I was often on the receiving end of his sharp tongue.

Douglas met my grandmother in Eastbourne, when he had changed careers once more and begun working for an abattoir, Baldocks, in the village of Wivelsfield. Because of his job my grandparents were able to get a 'tied house' owned by the abattoir. It was nothing special – a typical cottage with an outside toilet and no bathroom – but they raised their family there.

Sadly, my grandmother Fry couldn't carry girls. She miscarried a number of girls. If she'd had them she would have had twelve children, apparently. My dad, Arthur Fry, was the fourth of five boys. It seems that they looked the spitting image of the boys on the old Fry's Five Boys chocolate bar, even though they were no relation to the confectionery family.

At the outbreak of war in 1939 the slaughterhouse was regarded as a military target. My grandfather and grandmother had three boys at that point, with another on the way. The three boys were evacuated while my grandmother remained at home to have her baby. My grandfather was exempt from military service. By then, not only was he a slaughter man, he was also a driver and was considered important to the war effort because he used to drive the meat lorries up to Smithfield Market in London. He apparently drove through the Blitz on several occasions.

At first my grandmother remained at home. But as the intensity of the German raids on southern England increased, it was decided that she should also be evacuated to Cirencester. She was pregnant with my father at the time. So it was there, at the Sunnyside nursing home, that on 21 October 1940 –Trafalgar Day – she gave birth to my father, Arthur. His being born on Trafalgar Day gave my grandmother the mad idea to call him Horatio Nelson but, thankfully for him, my grandfather stepped in and said that was daft and insisted he was christened Arthur Frederick instead. In a way, that typified the two sides of my grandfather. He had actually been christened Arthur Douglas but insisted on being known as Douglas because he hated the name Arthur. Yet even though he didn't like the name, he gave it to his fourth son. Strange.

My father didn't remain in Cirencester for long. He was only a few weeks old when my grandmother decided that she didn't like being billeted with the very old and grouchy lady with whom she had been forced to share a bed. She was so homesick she couldn't stand it. So, with the few shillings she had, she jumped on a train one day and took the day-long journey back to Haywards Heath railway station. From there she walked with her baby in her arms all the way back to Wivelsfield. To my grandfather's astonishment, she walked back through the door and in no uncertain terms informed him that she didn't care if she was bombed, she wasn't leaving her home again. She was clearly made of strong stuff – as she proved once more shortly after that.

Having returned home with my father, she decided that she was going to put the whole family back together. It's funny how this is a recurring theme in both my families. As was the case with my great-uncles, when they rescued my other grandmother from an asylum, Freda showed a very similar mix of spirit, determination – and ingenuity. She wrote to the Home Office to check on the three boys' whereabouts, but there was some confusion and they couldn't find them at first. This wasn't good enough for my grand-mother, so out of desperation she wrote a letter to one of the most famous women in England at the time: Lady Nancy Astor, the first woman MP. It must have been one heck of a letter. Not only did Nancy Astor receive the letter, she replied to it – with a personal visit to my grandmother's house. Driven by her chauf-feur and sitting in a gas-powered car, Nancy Astor came down from the House of Commons to this little house in Wivelsfield where, over a cup of tea and some home-made cakes no doubt, she promised my grand-mother that she would get her children back for her. She was as good as her word. Within two weeks the three older sons were back home. I wish we still had that letter. Sadly, my grandmother only told me this story very late in her life. I wonder how it might have affected my relationship with my paternal grandfather if I had known this story earlier.

The two sides of my family lived several miles apart from each other, but in one of those strange moments of synchronicity, their paths did cross.

Towards the end of the war, when my father was about three years of age, my grandmother was taken ill and my father had to be temporarily taken into a care home. He didn't go very far; he went to Eastbourne. By a really strange coincidence, my mother was sent to the exact same home at the same time because her mother was also ill. It was only during the early years of their marriage, when they began talking about their wartime experiences, that they realised the coincidence. The thing that confirmed they must have been in the same place at around the same time was they both remem-bered the fact that there had been a tortoise living there.

My parents' paths diverged pretty wildly during their childhoods in the 1950s. My father left school early and got a job working as a farmhand on a chicken and dairy farm in Wivelsfield. He didn't ven-ture far from the family's home at all – unlike my mother, who wandered a little too far at times.

I think it's fair to say that my mother was a bit of a wild child. When she was around fourteen years old, she and a friend decided that they wanted to visit France. So they stowed away on a train to Portsmouth and got on a cross channel ferry with no passport. Of course, they got no further than passport control in France where they were taken into custody and plonked straight on the next ferry back across the English Channel. They were brought home by the police. It caused a huge fuss, apparently, with the local authorities getting involved.

My mother was so wilful that it was decided she should be sent to live with her aunt and uncle for a while, to calm her down. My grandmother was ill at the time with pernicious anaemia and really couldn't cope with her high-spirited daughter. So my mother was sent to live with her Uncle Charlie and Auntie Vera in London.

She had the time of her life, it seems. My mum was there during the time of the coffee bars and the birth of rock 'n' roll. She dated Tommy Steele's brother Colin for a while. It was a family joke that I was named after him, whereas in fact I was named after a famous cricketer. I have no idea why – my dad wasn't a cricket fan. I think they just liked the name.

Later, my mother dated Norman Linton Jr for a short time. After the war utility clothes were quite popular. Norman Linton was the market leader and made fashionable clothes for ladies. Norman Jr was his son and heir, and he wanted to marry my mother but she wasn't interested.

It took an accident on the streets of London to slow my mother down – and bring her back to the Sussex countryside. When she was sixteen she was running to jump on a bus when she slipped and fell on the pavement really heavily, hurting her spine badly. Many years later a doctor told her that it was something of a miracle that she'd been able to carry children at all because of the damage the accident had caused.

In the wake of the accident, my mother returned home. It was then that she met my father. They were both in their late teens. By the time they were approaching their twenty-first birthdays, they had decided they wanted to marry. This, of course, was a bit of a problem in those days because you needed parental consent to marry before you had 'come of age' at twenty-one. At first, both sets of parents objected. They thought they were too young. But they were obviously persuasive and managed to get married in March of 1961, a month ahead of my mother's twenty-first in April and seven months ahead of my father's in October. They got married in Wivelsfield. It was snowing that day, apparently – and the atmosphere would have been distinctly chilly inside the church too, I can imagine. My grandmother, Lilian, disapproved very strongly of the fact that her daughter was getting married in a non-Catholic church. The nuns' influence over her remained strong, it seems.

Life was difficult for my parents, as it was for most young newlyweds without much money to their name back then. They went on honeymoon to the Isle of Wight. My father got some grit in his eye on the ferry and had to wear an eye-patch through the whole honeymoon. In the first weeks of their marriage, they lodged with an old lady in Wivelsfield. It was an arrangement that my mother hated.

My father had originally been a farmhand on a chicken and dairy farm, but my mother objected to the early starts and late finishes, so he took up an apprenticeship with a company called Frank White & Sons as a painter and decorator. Again, family history seemed to be repeating itself, and they were given one of the houses that Mr White rented out. It was a small two-bedroom Victorian terraced cottage. I can still remember the address: 1, Clifton Cottages, Petlands Gardens, Haywards Heath. It had no bathroom, only an outside toilet with a willow pattern on it. There was no roof on the toilet so you had to take an umbrella out with you.

My mother was a student nurse and to make up a little bit of extra money my father used to work a couple of nights a week in a local pub. Their plan was to wait for five years before having children so that they could save up for the expense. Well, the best laid plans . . .

In August 1961, having just got settled into their new home where the landlord was building a new kitchen and an inside toilet for them, my mother discovered that she was pregnant. Apparently she was so furious that she didn't speak to my father for three weeks. My father on the other hand was ecstatic that they were going to have a baby.

The truth was that my mother understood the practicalities of it all. She knew the imminent arrival of a baby meant that she would have to give up nursing and that money was going to be even tighter than usual. To minimise the impact my arrival would have on them, she carried on working until she was eight months pregnant.

2 | Angels

I MAY not always have been an easy child, but apparently I was a very easy birth. I was born on 19 May 1962 at around 1.30 pm at Cuckfield Hospital on the outskirts of Haywards Heath. The first person to see me was my grandfather Lawrie. He was a kitchen porter at the hospital at the time. I think my dad went in when he finished work, which was the norm in those days.

My mum took a year or so off work to raise me but got very bad postnatal depression and took the decision to return to nursing. So, for large parts of the time, the job of raising me went to her mother, my grandmother Lilian.

My mother used to work three days a week and also nights. When my mum was working day-shifts, my grandmother spent the day with me. When she was working the nightshift, Lilian would be with me until my mum got up at three in the afternoon. I can still remember us walking around the house trying to be quiet while my mum slept.

That was the way it was for me from the age of

eighteen months until I was nine or so. It had an enormous impact on me, not least because my grandmother had a psychic ability and, in her own particular way, allowed me to develop the strange abilities I had already begun demonstrating.

The first time these abilities had shown themselves had been when I was in my cot, apparently. My mother had put me down for the night, knowing that she'd have to get up during the small hours to feed me later. But when she had come into the nursery to check on me, to her surprise she discovered me awake, gurgling away quite happily. She swears that suspended above my cot was a baby's rattle. It was rattling in the air but the moment she stepped towards me it just dropped back into the cot.

I have no memory of that incident at all. My earliest 'normal' memory is of me standing up in what used to be the dining area of our little house. I was in a nappy, and the floor was concrete. I can remember there being a tarpaulin covering up building work that was going on. I recall walking quickly but then hearing my mother shouting at me and dropping back to my bottom. Apparently they had been my first steps, but rather than being elated my mother had been terrified because there had been all this building work. I got the message: I didn't walk again for another three months, by which time the building work was complete.

My first memory of my being an unusual child,

however, came a year or so after that, when we went to see Father Christmas for the first time. I would have been two or two and a half years old. I was taken to Wade's department store in Brighton. In those days the grottos were spectacular. I remember going with my dad, mum and my grandparents on my mother's side, Lilian and Lawrie.

There was a rather lovely nativity scene and Lawrie had pointed at this figure and said, 'Oh, look, that's an angel.' I remember clearly that I said, 'No, that's not what an angel looks like.'

Another memory, from about a year later, when I was three, offers further evidence that I was already seeing things that other people were not. At that time my best friend was the girl next door, Debbie Stafford. Our families were very close and so I often used to see her parents, whom I used to call Uncle Ken and Auntie Edith. Their house always seemed to be in a state of disrepair, with building work going on. But Debbie and I constantly played together at each other's houses.

One day we were playing while Uncle Ken was building behind the back door. He had built some kind of wall and there was this big drop of about five or six feet onto the ground at the rear of the house. Debbie and I were riding around the house on a tricycle and we somehow cycled towards where Ken was building and fell off, right over the edge. I can still vividly remember it. To a three-year-old child, at least, it looked like a precipice – like I was falling off the end of the earth.

Debbie grazed her knee, but I hit my head really hard, so hard in fact that I ended up with a cut on my chin which left a scar that I still have to this day. There was blood everywhere, apparently.

It was decided that I needed to go to hospital. They were worried I'd banged my head so hard that I had sustained brain damage. It was all very dramatic: I remember lying in my grandmother's arms while my mother ran down the road to the telephone box to call for an ambulance. It was then that I saw something extraordinary.

As things calmed down I was suddenly aware that I could see all these people standing behind my grandmother. There were more people than I could possibly count. And they were all glowing a luminescent white. We were surrounded by them. 'Nanny, I can see all the angels,' I told my grandmother. 'But it's all right because the angels are touching me now, so I know I am going to be better.'

It was probably my first profound clairvoyant experience. I wasn't frightened by the figures I saw there. It seemed normal; it just didn't feel peculiar.

What was interesting about this was my grandmother's reaction. She said, 'Colin, you've banged your head, be quiet.' Even at that age I could sense a slight hint of panic in her voice. I know now that it was because she understood all too well what I was seeing. And she understood it because she had experienced unusual things like this herself.

There was no doubt in my mind that Lilian had inherited her mother Minnie's gifts.

I remember when she used to knit and she had a large bag full of different coloured wools. Whenever she dipped down into the bag to fish out a new ball of wool, she wouldn't need to look down. She would always pull out the right colour. I remember asking her about this once and she said to me: 'I have eyes in my hands, I can see through my hands.'

It was clear it was not a joke.

As we spent most of our days together, my grandmother and I developed a special way of communicating. We used to have conversations without talking. I would send her a thought, asking for a drink or a biscuit perhaps. Without saying a word, she would get up get me what I had asked for and give it to me with a smile. I thought it was normal. Of course, it wasn't – and she knew it.

I felt like I could say anything to my grandmother. So, as I got a little older, and I began to see the figure of an old, grey-haired man sitting at the bottom of my bed, I had no qualms about telling her. My favourite programme on the TV at the time was *Dr Who*, starring William Hartnell, and I can remember saying to her that the man I saw looked like a taller, slightly thinner version of William Hartnell. It would take me many years to discover who that man really was.

There is no doubt in my mind that my grandmother was scared of her gift. It wasn't just the incident when I told her I could see angels. I often sensed her unease when I spoke of the things I could see. We never spoke about it in depth, but I think the Catholic influence in her life was the root cause. So for that reason, our special relationship remained our little secret. No one else knew about it; well, so we thought.

My early childhood was a happy one, but it was tinged with sadness too. One day, when I was aged three, I walked into the bathroom to find my mother lying on the floor, obviously in distress. As I looked down, I saw there was a pool of blood next to her. I was terrified but she told me there was no need to worry. 'Colin, I want you to go next door and get Auntie Cathy,' she said to me, calmly.

Cathy was an Irish lady who lived next door. She was also my godmother and one of my mother's best friends. I squeezed my way through a hole in the fence and ran to Cathy's kitchen. 'Cathy, come quick – my mummy is on the bathroom floor,' I said and almost made Cathy drop the saucepan she was holding.

Cathy looked shocked for a second but soon gathered herself and grabbed some towels before running back to our house with me. I was told in no uncertain terms to stay in the dining room. As a three-year-old I couldn't have comprehended fully what happened, but somehow, the idea that my mum had lost a baby – and that it was a girl – was embedded in my mind. It stayed there for many years.

My parents clearly decided to try for another child and when I was five a baby arrived safely. This time it was a boy, a brother. I confess I was disappointed because I wanted a sister. I reduced my mum to tears when she came home from hospital, cradling this vulnerable little baby, named Glenn. I remember I had just started school and had walked in at the end of the day to discover a crowd of people in the front lounge. There was a cot there. I guessed it was something special. We never used the front lounge, except at the weekends. Apart from Christmas and weekends we lived in the back dining room. They also had the gas fire on, which, again, we never did normally.

Everyone was smiling and my father gave me a present that I was told was from my new little brother. It was a car, a Corgi Batmobile. I wasn't impressed by it, nor by my brother.

'Aren't you going to say hello to Glenn,' my dad asked.

'No, I'm not. He's ugly,' I apparently replied.

It had been quite a difficult birth and Glenn was quite bruised, so my unfeeling words set my mother off into a flood of tears and I was rushed out of the room.

Looking back on it, I can see that it was a normal reaction from a first-born child who was used to having the run of the house. I could sense that my place at the centre of the home was in danger. But I think it was also rooted in the fact that I'd already begun to feel like I'd become an outcast from that home, sentenced to daily incarceration at the awful prison that was school.

3 | Kicking and Screaming

THEY say that schooldays are the best days of your
life; well, for me they were the complete opposite.
I hated the whole experience from the day I started at
primary school at the age of five to the day I left secondary school at the age of fifteen. There were moments
when it was tolerable and I met some teachers and
other children with whom I was friendly, but in general
I absolutely loathed it.

My mother wanted me to go to the same school as
she had done, so I went to New England Road
Primary School a couple of miles from our house.
Those first days as a young schoolboy are still etched
on my memory. I had to wear a tie, blazer and cap,
and a pair of shorts that left my legs exposed to the
elements. I can still remember having to walk in the
freezing rain and wind during some bitterly cold win-
ters. It's funny looking back on my childhood in the
Sussex countryside: I can't remember a winter without snow and rain and high winds.

As for school, the memories of New England Road
Primary are just as strong. I can still remember the

smell of dust and floor polish. The slightly rancid smell of the small bottle of lukewarm milk that we were given every morning. School was an alien environment, one in which I didn't really feel I belonged.

The shock of being removed from the safe, loving environment of my home to school was huge. A couple of times I ran away, chasing my mother home after she'd dropped me off in the morning. I had to be dragged back to school, literally kicking and screaming.

During my first years at school we had two teachers who job-shared, one was called Miss Hilton and the other was Miss Simmonds. I quite liked Miss Simmonds but not Miss Hilton. She was a big woman who terrified me.

Part of the problem was that I wasn't very good at lessons. I am instinctively left-handed which, in those days, was forbidden, so they were always trying to get me to do things with my right hand. But I wasn't stupid. I could read before I started school; however, I couldn't write because they kept making me swap hands. (Consequently, I am now ambidextrous.)

Another big problem was the fact that I didn't understand anything, and I also didn't see the point of it. I was a child who lived on his imaginative abilities. I was also the child who always asked: 'Why?' For example, every day before we went home we'd sit on the floor in a circle and Miss Hilton would get a cardboard clock out and set the hands. We would have to tell the time. I could never get it right. To me it was pointless; I only needed to know mealtimes and when it was time to go home, which I could instinctively do. So I would ask, 'Why do I need to know that?' and 'Why do I need to know this?' And the reply was always the same: 'Because you need to know.' Well, to me that was never a good enough answer.

Even at that early age, I sensed that school wasn't going to teach me anything I wanted to know. I felt that my education was going to come in another environment.

I was far more preoccupied with playing games with Debbie next door, something that I did on an almost daily basis. Again, this fed my imagination much more than school ever did. We would play make-believe games in which I would be the King and she would be the Queen, or I was Dr Who and she was my assistant. Also, my dad had bought me a Bazooka Joe rocket launcher and built me a wooden go-kart. I could spend hours playing with those. They – and the people I could see that nobody else could – were the important things in life. School was an imposition. My life became a matter of how many days it was until the weekend.

Interestingly, I didn't mind going to Sunday school at our local Methodist Chapel. It was run by two ladies and I quite enjoyed the whole of experience, because I liked the stories. That tied in with the other experiences I was having. I loved colouring in Jesus and his disciples, and the Nativity and angels in particular. Of course, no one understood why I felt so connected to the subject.

I was continuing to see and hear things that other people could not. At that point, I didn't realise the importance of keeping quiet about my abilities and would occasionally come out with an unusual comment or two. Of course, people would look at me strangely when we were talking about Jesus and the angels and I would just casually say: 'Oh yes, I know – I can see angels.' But, at that point, they just dismissed it as the sweet ramblings of an imaginative young boy. I don't think anyone at Sunday school could possibly have suspected that I was a young psychic.

My mother, on the other hand, was getting an inkling that there was something unusual going on. One day – it must have been during a school holiday or a weekend – a friend came round to the house to see my mother. I'd kept a polite silence and stayed in my room while the two women had a cup of tea and a chat. At one point, however, I'd not been able to resist taking a peek into the living room and had been amazed to see that there was a little boy standing there, who was being totally ignored by both my mother and her visitor, who I assumed was his mother. He had curly, ginger-coloured hair and looked a bit peeved. He was even tugging on his mother's coat at one point, but she didn't react at all.

When they left I asked my mother why they'd treated him like that.

My mother had looked baffled. 'What are you talking about, Colin? What little boy?' she'd said. When I described him in great detail her face turned white. She then produced an old shoebox in which she kept a pile of fading photographs and pulled out a photograph of a boy, whom I immediately identified.

'Yes, that's him,' I said.

'That's her son, John. He died five years before you were born,' she said.

If only school had been as interesting as the spirit world seemed to be. But I did have a friend there, Malcolm Piper. I was small but he was even smaller. The other thing we had in common was that we both suffered from asthma. My condition wasn't helped by the cold. Our house was so cold that my mother had to put polythene sheets on the inside of the old sash windows because ice used to form there. There was always a paraffin heater on the half landing to generate some warmth because the cold made my asthma bad. They would keep my bed propped up and make sure I always had tons of Vicks rubbed into my chest but even then they had to call the doctor out to the house a couple of times because I was having trouble breathing.

Malcolm and I were fellow sufferers, the weaklings of the school, I suppose. That formed a bond between us. However, he and his family emigrated to Australia. I often wonder what became of him.

As I grew up and moved through the years at

school, I continued to struggle. Looking back on it, I can see I was bright and intelligent enough, but that it didn't come out in the work that I did. It was because I had no interest. It was no great surprise when I was put in a remedial class, which I actually loved. It may well have been the only spell at school that I truly enjoyed. I was taught by a teacher called Miss Balls, who was the first teacher to stimulate my interest. She had taught my mother too and was quite elderly. She was considered old school and strict, but I really liked her.

Miss Balls opened up lots possibilities to me that I hadn't had in the main class. Three days a week she would read to us and she would always choose really great books like *Swallows and Amazons* or *Treasure Island*, which encouraged me to read too. I would have been six or seven by then. With Miss Balls' encouragement, I started to read the classics and from then on reading was my great passion – I read all the time. She also taught us stitching and how to make raffia baskets and stuff like that. I loved it all. And she got me interested in drawing too, but not just sloshing paint on paper. She would ask us to copy a vase of flowers.

Of course, nothing lasts forever and Miss Balls retired midway through my schooldays when I was about eight years old. She was replaced by Miss George, who soon realised that I shouldn't really be in a remedial class. I remember that once she asked us to write a poem which I didn't really want to do. At the time there was a song called 'Little Green Apples' by Roger Miller, which my dad really liked. We had the record and played it on the gramophone. As I didn't want to write a poem I wrote down the lyrics for 'Little Green Apples' instead – and I got a gold star for it.

A few days later I was asked to see the headmaster, Mr Perrin, with my mother. Back then, you only saw the headmaster at assembly or if you were in trouble – and I'd never been in trouble. The headmaster and Miss George said they were going to move me to another class. I was really upset. I didn't want to move. The new class was run by a Miss Hopkins. And it turned out that it was the best thing that ever happened to me, because she introduced me to drama. I loved getting the big roles in the school pantomime. I played the cook in *Alice in Wonderland* once: it was my first experience in drag and I got rave reviews. Miss Hopkins was great and I even began to grasp maths with her guidance. She would make us recite tables in the morning and one day while we were doing this I suddenly realised that I knew it, that it had clicked into place in my mind. Two fourteens are twenty-eight. I think I was around nine at the time.

The sense that I had a really unusual ability began to take root around the time I was approaching ten years of age. As I headed towards the final years of my junior school I began to understand just how different

I was from the other children and that I had a special kind of connection to the spirit world. I regularly heard voices and saw people that others clearly couldn't see. In particular, the old white-haired Dr Who lookalike appeared every now and again at the foot of my bed.

By now I had also begun to experience other things beyond simply seeing angels. There was one particular voice that I started to hear every now and again. It was that of a youngish woman, and she would always say the same thing: 'Not long.' I know now that it was the voice of my great-grandmother, Granny Lilian's mother Minnie. But I didn't know it then.

The first time I can remember hearing it was perhaps the most significant. I have touched upon the events surrounding my grandfather Lawrie's passing before, in earlier books. Those events changed me and my life forever. What I have not revealed until now, however, is that the woman's voice warned of his passing days earlier.

What happened was this: I had been vaguely aware that my grandfather Lawrie was not well. He had just retired, having reached the age of sixty-five, after a life-time spent doing menial jobs. He had never been the healthiest of men. He had suffered from a back deformity and was blind in one eye. But as I'd been going through junior school I had noticed that his health had clearly deteriorated. By the time I was ten he had lost weight and was looking extremely drawn. The truth was that he was suffering from cancer. In retrospect, I find it extremely sad that the man who had asked for so little from life would be dead within a year of retirement.

My brother was too young to understand what was happening and I had been protected from this for a long time. But it was when I was taken to see him at the old Bevendean Hospital in Brighton that it really struck home.

It was, I'm pretty sure, the first time I had been to visit anyone in hospital. So it was the first time that I experienced that awful smell. I think it was the first time that I smelled death.

As I was walking down the hospital corridor with my parents, I heard the woman's voice. 'Not long,' she said in a voice that was at the same time soft and whispered, but also distinctive and real. At first I imagined it had come from somewhere else and looked around to see who had spoken. But, apart from my parents and a couple of male porters wheeling empty beds around, there was no one there.

As soon as I saw my grandfather I knew that there was something seriously wrong with him and that he couldn't have long to live. It had been a couple of weeks since I'd seen him and in that time he had deteriorated even more. His skin had become almost translucent and blue. But he managed to give me a weak smile and squeeze my hand. He called me 'Sonny Boy', which was his favourite term of endearment for me. I left the hospital sensing that I might have seen him for the last time. I was only half right.

Within a day or so of my visit they transferred him up to London, to Charing Cross Hospital, to try to perform an operation that they couldn't do at Bevendean. A few days later, one night when I was being looked after by my paternal grandparents, I received a visit from Lawrie in my bedroom. My brother was fast asleep in the bed next to me and oblivious to it all. Lawrie sat there and spoke to me about how he was feeling much better and had come to say goodbye. He promised me that he would remain with me in spirit and would appear to me again, but that no one else would see me in the same way.

'It will just be you and me, Sonny Boy,' he'd said.

Afterwards I'd gone down to see my grandparents and told them Lawrie had been to see me and had said goodbye. Their reaction had been immediate: my grandfather had angrily told me to go back to bed.

It was only the following day, when my parents returned from London, that the reality sank in. My mother had, apparently, been upset when my grandparents had told her that I already knew of Lawrie's passing. She imagined they had woken me up to tell me after she'd telephoned them with the news in the middle of the night.

My mother had turned as white as a sheet when my grandmother Freda told her that it was in fact the other way around: I had told them.

Lawrie was true to his word and would return to guide me again in my life, appearing frequently over the coming years. But during the period immediately following his passing he was less present, which I now know to be because of the transition process we go through when we first enter the spirit world.

But the voice of the woman didn't go away. In fact I heard it again twice in the coming months.

The next time I heard it, it was connected to a friend of my mother's. By this time, my mother had taken a break from nursing and was working as a cook at a local Catholic school. Because she had to leave so early for work, I would go with her and sit in the staff room until it was time for me to walk a few hundred yards round the corner to my own school. I didn't really know this friend of my mother's well, but she was sitting drinking tea in the school kitchen when I heard the words once more: 'Not long.' I recognised the distinctive voice immediately.

To be honest, I don't think I'd understood the significance of the 'not long' I'd heard that first time at Bevendean Hospital. The experience of visiting my grandfather in hospital, and then having him visit me on the night he died, had been too overwhelming. I hadn't been able to take stock.

This time it was different. Later that week, I found my mother and her colleagues in the school kitchen. The ladies were devastated as they had been told that their friend had passed away suddenly from a heart attack. A thought began to crystallise for the first time. Was the voice a warning, a premonition of death? It wasn't long before I had it confirmed for certain.

At primary school there was a boy who I'll call Tim, who was in the same class as me. We were sitting in class one day when I heard that voice again, saying, 'Not long.' This time I thought I really must be mistaken. 'That can't be right,' I remember saying to myself. 'Little boys don't die.' I guessed it must be a teacher at the school, a man called Mr Claridge.

So I dismissed it to the back of my mind until about a fortnight later, when I saw a couple of female teachers crying one morning. I noticed that Tim wasn't at school that day and asked about him. I was told that it wasn't my concern and to get on with my work. It was obvious that something awful had happened and I could sense that he had died. No announcement was made at school, however. As the days passed and Tim's chair at school remained empty, it was as if he had been airbrushed out of existence.

My parents didn't know his family, so information was slow in coming. Eventually, someone who knew a teacher confirmed that Tim wouldn't be coming back to school again. He had died very suddenly of a cerebral haemorrhage.

As a young boy growing up and trying to find his place in the world, these sorts of events were difficult for me.

On the one hand, my mother and grandmother were both cautioning me to be careful about letting people know about my abilities. On the other hand, I had begun to experience profound things. I had had my eyes opened to the possibility that I could foretell people's death and converse with those who had passed over.

The temptation was to keep quiet, to shut it out of my mind, especially at school where I sensed it could get me into a lot of trouble. That was easier said than done of course, especially where other children were concerned.

Around about this time we moved house. In the wake of my grandfather's passing it had been decided that my grandmother Lilian would move in with us, so we had needed a larger home with an extra bedroom. We had moved to a house in America Lane which is a continuation of New England Road, so much nearer to the school. We moved there during the summer before my final year at primary school.

I'd been a bit worried about it but had been reassured by my grandfather Lawrie. While I was out walking near our new home one day, I sensed his presence close to me. He told me that I was going to be very happy in this new home and that I shouldn't worry. He was right.

From the social point of view, the move to a new home was good news for me. It was a less rural location than our old home and I made new friends immediately. In particular, I befriended twin brothers,

Peter and Stephen Cottington, who introduced me to their gang. It was my first experience of male bonding. Until then my best friend had been the girl next door. I had never had male friends. I was tiny so they took me under their wing. I began to use my talents to cement my place in the gang. They especially liked it when I told them ghost stories.

In those days parents would go off to work and leave you to your own devices as long as there was an adult around to keep a general eye on all of us. So we would go round to each other's houses. It was safe, whereas today it's 'don't talk to strangers', 'don't light fires', 'don't do this or do that'.

We boys would sit in a lounge and draw the curtains. Then I would scare the living daylights out of them. I used to love the Pan book of ghost stories, so I would read stories like 'The Monkey's Paw' and then make up my own versions of it. It was a little like the gang of boys in Stephen King's wonderful boyhood memoir *Stand By Me*, in which one of the boys would use his gift for storytelling around the campfire. Sometimes I would incorporate things in my stories about what I'd experienced on a psychic level. For instance, I would tell stories about what happens when you die. They were fascinated by me, but also a little bit scared.

It was around this time that something else began to happen. My mother had a friend – I think her name was Joan – who she used to work with, and who was a very distinctive-looking woman with an even more distinctive taste in clothes and accessories. She had a crocodile handbag with a crocodile head on it. She would often pop in for a cup of tea and a gossip with my mother when she was off work. Back in those days you were expected to be quiet and stay out of the way when someone came to visit your parents. But I remember that on this one occasion I overheard my mother and Joan talking. I heard Joan say that she'd been to some kind of meeting where there had been something called a medium who gave messages from the dead.

I made up an excuse to be in the kitchen and eavesdropped some more. Joan described how she'd been at a meeting where a woman had received a message from her departed mother. The medium was a man and had gone into a trance. He had then begun speaking in a woman's voice, apparently identical to that of the woman's mother. 'It was amazing,' Joan said. 'I spoke to the lady afterwards and she said it was as if she was in the room with her.'

I thought this was interesting. It sounded like it related to the experiences I'd been having since I was young. I decided to take a risk and chipped into the conversation.

'Excuse me, but is it not normal for people to see dead people?' I said, as politely as possible. Joan looked at my mum and my mum looked back at her.

They both smiled and then Joan said: 'No, it's not, only a few people have the gift and are able to do it.'

'Oh, I see,' I said, realising from the glare my mother was beginning to give me that I'd better not push it too far.

I left the kitchen with my mind racing. Maybe this was what I was? Maybe this explained what I could do? It wasn't long afterwards that I became convinced that it was.

As part of our regular meetings, our gang had started to do more and more 'spooky' things. By now, I had discovered that I somehow had the power to make strange things happen. In my bedroom I had discovered that, if I concentrated hard enough, I could make objects move; in particular, I could make the lightshade that hung from the ceiling swing around.

I had shown my friends this once and they had been amazed. This had, of course, given me a lot of kudos within the group and – kids being kids – things had progressed from there. Uri Geller had begun to get a bit of publicity around this time and one day my gang and some other kids were sitting on the local green, talking about him.

'How can he bend spoons?' someone had said. 'That's impossible.'

'No, it isn't,' I said, for no reason. 'I can do all that.'

'Yeah, yeah, yeah,' said one of the girls who was sitting with us.

'Yes, I can. I can even mend broken watches,' I

said, again for reasons not even known to myself.

'All right then,' the girl said. 'Wait there.' Sure enough, she went off then reappeared with an old broken watch of her father's. I was worried that I wasn't going to be able to do anything, so I asked my grandfather for help. I laid my hands on the watch and squeezed as hard as I could. No one was more amazed than me when it started working.

'What else can you do, what else can you do?' they'd all shouted.

'I can make lampshades swing,' I said. We were soon sitting in another friend's empty living room as I successfully put into practice the 'trick' I'd learned in my bedroom.

All this took place during the summer holidays, when we'd left primary school. A lot of us were going our separate ways and took advantage of hanging out together for what we thought might be the final time.

One particular summer's evening, we decided to make a Ouija board. Someone had been reading about these boards and was convinced that we could 'talk to the dead' through it. One of the gang found a photograph of one, which we reproduced using Lexicon cards. That evening after dark, we settled down to see what we could glean from it. No sooner had we sat down than I suddenly felt quite light-headed. The next thing I knew, I was coming round with the Cottington twins and the others all gathered around me.

'How did you do that, Colin?' one of them asked.

'How did I do what?' I replied, genuinely at a loss to know what they were talking about.

'Your eyes went all funny and then suddenly you were talking in the voice of an old man. You scared the living daylights out of us.'

'I have no idea what you are talking about,' I said, deliberately lying. My mind had immediately flashed back to the overheard conversation in my mother's kitchen. I had a very strong idea about what had happened.

We all headed home that night sworn to secrecy, vowing that we wouldn't tell our parents what we'd been up to. I, more than any of them, made certain that I stuck to that promise.

4 | **Playing with Fire**

IN the autumn of 1972 I headed off, with a heavy heart, to secondary school. I'd got a place at a comprehensive school in Haywards Heath, which was called Scrace Bridge when I started. However, at some point during that first year at the school the headmaster changed its name. It became Oathall Secondary School, now Oathall Community College. Apparently he thought the old name sounded too much like the word 'disgrace', which wasn't far short of the truth. By all accounts it is a very good school now. It certainly wasn't back then.

I must have stuck out like a sore thumb as a 'new boy'. I was still a lot smaller than the other children in my year: about four foot two, which was really short for an eleven-year-old. I probably weighed no more than four and a half stone. On top of that, parents in those days had this thing of buying you uniforms that 'you grew into'. So I headed off to school on my first day with trousers that were a bit too long because 'I would grow into them' and a jumper that was a bit baggy because 'I would grow into it'. For the same reason I had to turn up the sleeves of my blazer. As if that wasn't enough, I had a big latch-top briefcase that was almost half my size. So that accentuated my smallness even more. I must have made quite a sight.

My biggest fear during my first days was that I would have to go through some kind of initiation ceremony. There was a rumour at primary school that on your first day at secondary school, the older boys would get hold of you and 'bog wash' you. It was a story put around by those who had already made the move up to secondary. They would tell tales of how a gang of big, physically-intimidating older boys would somehow get hold of you and stick your head down the toilet.

It was a myth, of course. It didn't happen. But it didn't make the first few weeks any less intimidating an experience. I was terrified for most of the time, especially of the bullies.

It is only when you go to secondary school that you become aware of bullying. It didn't really exist in primary school. In primary school, there were only naughty children or bad children and if they pushed you over or did something mean to you there was a supervisor or teacher there to tell them off. But this was different. There were some really rough kids at the school, a lot of them from a large council estate nearby. I heard blood-curdling tales of how they would rob and attack kids on the way to and from school. I kept my wits about me and managed to avoid them somehow.

As if the threat of bigger children wasn't enough, there was the PE lesson to contend with. Ours was a football and gymnastics school. It was also a school that placed great store on cross-country running. I will never forget the experience of being in shorts on a freezing morning, having to do what was known as the bog trot – a cross-country run which would leave you completely caked in mud. I was also still mildly asthmatic so the whole thing was purgatory for me. There was also an outdoor swimming pool, which was freezing. We always seemed to start swimming in the middle of winter. That was one aspect of secondary school that I particularly loathed and detested.

Fortunately, I had my grandfather in particular to guide me. Every now and again, when the fear was threatening to overwhelm me, I would feel his calming presence. Once or twice, as I hauled my oversized briefcase to school, waiting for the moment when the gangs would jump and rob me, I heard him say, 'Don't worry, Sonny Boy – you'll be fine.' And he was right – well, for a while at least.

Throughout this time, in part thanks to my grandfather, I was continuing to explore my unusual abilities. After the incident with the Ouija board, I had decided to keep it as private as possible. So, alone in my room at home, I would practise making the lampshades move or concentrate so that small objects jumped or slid across the desk in my room. I had also learned how to make a small ball of light appear and move around at will. It was a matter of using my mind correctly: I would think it and it would go where I wanted it to go.

At the same time I started reading more and more about the psychic world, heading down to the local library to read the ghost, paranormal and psychic research books they had there. I would never be allowed to take them out, so I would spend hours poring over them in the evenings and at weekends. There were a couple of books in particular that interested me, one by a lady called Florence Marryat with the title *Researches in the Phenomena of Spiritualism* (1894) and another by Nandor Fodor called *The Encyclopaedia of Psychic Science*.

The more I read, and the more I learned about the abilities I had, the more I came to see what a huge responsibility I had been given. I knew I had to tread very carefully. I also knew that I had a lot to learn.

One of most important lessons I got during that period, appropriately enough, came within school itself and involved a French teacher. She was a younger teacher, a very warm person and very encouraging of my work. One day, as we were all packing up our satchels at the end of the lesson, she asked me to stay behind. 'Don't worry, it's nothing bad, Colin, I'd just like to go through something you did in your home-work,' she smiled.

It was rare that I picked up on anything psychically

within school. I actively stopped myself from thinking that way for fear of what might happen. Fortunately, the atmosphere there was usually too noisy for me to have any chance to think about it in any case. As I stood in the suddenly empty classroom on this particular day, however, it was different. I was standing next to the French teacher at her desk, when I was suddenly aware of a really intense presence. I heard a very clear voice talking to me. It was an older woman, a spirit that I somehow sensed had passed over quite recently. For some reason, I felt I had to relay what she was saying.

'Monique wants to thank you for tying back her hair with yellow ribbon,' I said.

For a moment, I was terrified. What had I done?

I expected an instant reaction but instead the teacher went very quiet, continuing to look down at my exercise book. She then slowly raised her head, looked at me and said: 'Colin, how do you know that?'

'Because she's just told me,' I said.

Again, she took a moment or two to gather her thoughts. 'Colin, Monique is my mother,' she said. 'She died about a year ago.'

I just nodded.

'When I went to visit her for the last time in the Chapel of Rest, I tied her hair back with yellow ribbon,' she went on. 'How long have you done this?' she asked me.

'What?' I said, a little taken aback. At this point, I didn't really know what 'this' meant.

'Talk to dead people.'

'Oh, always,' I said, almost relieved that she had understood exactly what had happened.

She closed the French exercise book and asked me to sit down. 'Do your mum and dad know?' she asked.

'I think my mum knows, but we don't really talk about it,' I said.

She then said something that I have never forgotten. 'Colin, this is an amazing ability you have, and you are still a very young boy. But you might want to keep quiet about it until you're older.' This stopped me in my tracks. I realised she was right and that I had to be more careful about showing off what I was capable of doing. It wasn't something that I should treat as a piece of entertainment. It was a serious business, one that had the potential to help and heal people who were grieving the loss of loved ones.

The incident obviously made a big impression on her because my mother came back from a parents' evening not long afterwards and told me that she'd had a chat with my teacher. 'We had a very interesting conversation with your French teacher,' she said. 'You are not in trouble, but we'll talk about it sometime.'

My mother's attitude to the psychic side of my life continued to be very straightforward. She didn't encourage it particularly, but she didn't discourage it either. On that occasion she let me off with a gentle reminder to 'keep it under my hat'.

To be fair to her, my mother was doing her best to guide me. She knew she couldn't acknowledge my gift or do anything while my father was around. But when we had the house to ourselves, she would occasionally try things out with me. At one stage she began getting out photographs of old family members that I'd never met or pictures of friends of hers from years gone by. She'd place them face down on the kitchen counter. 'Tell me what you can about the people in this picture,' she'd say.

Curiously, my mother became friends with a woman with whom I had made the initial contact. Her name was Pat and she lived in a semi-detached house, with her husband and four kids, down a footpath that led from the back of our house. Pat fascinated me, partly because she looked so cool. She reminded me of Suzi Quatro and Julie Covington, the star of the big television series of the time, 'Rock Follies'. Pat had that same short cropped, pixie hair as Julie Covington and used to wear flared jeans and walk around barefoot. I think she even wore an Afghan coat. When I first went round to her house to check out some puppies that had been born, I saw that her home was full of esoteric ornaments, including a crystal ball. She was also burning sickly sweet-smelling joss sticks.

Pat and I became friends very quickly, and consequently she and my mother became friends as well. I seemed to be able to relate to Pat mainly because I sensed she had a rebellious spirit too. I had this instinct she would be interested, so almost as soon as I met her I told her about my being fascinated by mediumship and the psychic world. Sure enough, she was interested. 'Have you ever tried reading tarot cards?' she asked me that first time we spoke.

This sparked my curiosity and so I acquired a deck and started to teach myself tarot.

Through my mum's frienship with Pat, I felt I'd met an adult who understood me and with whom I could talk about my interests. We had numerous conversations in which we talked about Ouija boards and the dangers of using them. She also talked about Spiritualist churches, where mediums practised publicly, and told me there were a few of them in Brighton. I was determined I would visit one as soon as I could.

At that point, neither Pat, my mum nor I had a clue where all this was leading. But in later life Pat would play a very important part in my psychic development. To be fair, my mother wouldn't have had a clue how to guide me. She knew she couldn't acknowledge my gift while my father was around. Yet my abilities were simply a part of me that I wanted to explore. But the more I explored them the more obvious it was that I had a powerful gift. At times it' seemed almost too powerful.

My mother had an acquaintance called Audrey, who was pregnant at the time, and who asked me to do a tarot reading for her. This was something that I'd been studying for a year or two by now. I used them very sparingly with my mum and Pat or on my own.

'Your mum tells me that you read tarot,' Audrey said one evening when she was visiting. My father was out working at the pub. I shot my mother a concerned look and she nodded approvingly.

'Yes, I do,' I said.

'Could you give me a reading for the little one?' she said, patting her bump proudly.

I got out a set of cards that I had been given by Pat and laid them out. Audrey was sitting there watching me, but as I took a look at the cards splayed out in front of me, I could see absolutely nothing. It was bizarre in the extreme.

'Sorry Audrey, must be something I did,' I said, slightly panicked. 'Let me do it again.'

I shuffled the cards thoroughly then laid them out again. But the result was the same. Nothing. Not a single sign that connected anything together.

'Umm, this is embarrassing,' I said, by now looking at my mother for help.

'Maybe you are tired, Colin. Try one more time and if it doesn't work, then forget it and head off to bed.'

I shuffled the cards even more vigorously this time. I was determined to get a reading for Audrey, who was looking increasingly uncomfortable. 'OK, third time lucky,' I smiled, trying to make light of the situation. But it was no good. The third time it was exactly the same.

I apologised to Audrey and headed off to bed. To

be honest, I wasn't that concerned. I was still learning tarot and knew that it wasn't something that could be 'forced' to work. And I knew I had to be patient with the spirits that I was tapping into.

The next evening, I came downstairs to find my mother and father in the kitchen looking a bit shaken. 'What's wrong?' I said. 'What's happened?'

My father decided that he would be the bearer of the bad news. 'It's your mum's friend, Audrey,' he said, in a solemn voice. 'We've had some bad news about her. She's suffered a miscarriage. She's lost the baby.'

I knew I couldn't look at my mother because it would acknowledge that we were sharing some kind of secret. But I could sense her thoughts were exactly the same as mine: 'That's why the tarot cards showed nothing in the baby's future. In terms of this life, the baby didn't have one. The spirit world obviously knew it would soon be joining them.'

I wasn't quite sure what to think, but I knew how I felt. I wasn't frightened. But I was definitely shocked. A part of me was also confused. To begin with, I didn't understand why I hadn't heard the voice telling me 'not long'. I didn't understand why, on this occasion, the spirit world had delivered me a message in another way. I didn't understand how I was supposed to be able to interpret these things. I wasn't even sure whether I was *supposed* to understand these things.

My mother and I exchanged a brief word about it later that day when I got back from school, but she made it clear she didn't want me to talk about it again. To be honest, I was quite happy to comply.

For a while, in the aftermath of Audrey's loss, I had grave doubts about whether I should be dabbling in things I didn't fully understand. I felt like I was playing with fire. So, for a few months, I spent less time reading about those sorts of subjects and tried my best to put them out of my mind as much as possible. It seemed to me that the psychic world was too powerful, too complicated. It was too much for a teenager to cope with, especially given the other troubles that were brewing . . .

5 | Fighting Back

IT was becoming more and more obvious to me that school didn't hold the key to my future. It wasn't going to teach me about the kind of things I was really interested in. Owing to the numbing boredom of school life, I soon returned to my private study of the paranormal and all things spiritual – the subjects that really did fascinate me.

Instead, I felt that school was trying to mould me into something I was not. I was a square peg that they were trying to force into a round hole. I didn't belong there. That realisation only deepened as I entered my mid-teens and I increasingly became the victim of the school's bigots and bullies.

My first two years at school had been relatively trouble-free in terms of bullying. There was a large contingent of rough kids at school and I heard a lot about the violence they were doling out to some of the weaker kids. Until now I'd ridden my luck, but as I began my third year that luck began to run out.

In many ways, I stuck out even more now than I had done when I'd first arrived at school. I was small, sensitive and – at the age of thirteen – entering puberty, with all the confusing complications that come with it. In my case it was particularly complicated, of course. I suppose my emerging homosexuality was becoming apparent. By the standards of the time I was mildly effeminate and I was much more interested in talking to girls than boys. I certainly wasn't interested in the things that boys were supposed to be interested in.

Kids are perceptive and cruel, they find weaknesses in other children. So I became the target for that cruelty. It began with name-calling. Suddenly other boys were calling me poof and fairy. At this point I didn't even understand my sexuality myself, but their words struck a chord, of course. I had an inkling that I was 'different' sexually in the same way that I was psychically. I was certainly becoming aware of what homosexuality was.

I vividly remember that around about that time on television, they showed *The Naked Civil Servant* starring John Hurt as Quentin Crisp. It was a landmark moment for the gay community in the UK. It certainly was for me. Until now gay people on television had been nothing more than camp caricatures. I had seen the likes of Larry Grayson and John Inman on the box and I'd thought to myself, 'Well I'm like that, but I'm not like that.' Then I saw the Quentin Crisp story. I met him many years later when I went to a public performance. It was a profound and life-changing experience for me. Watching *The Naked Civil Servant* on television, I began to understand myself.

I didn't feel entirely alone. I had a strong feeling that there were other boys at school who felt the same as me. There was a boy in the class above me who was overtly effeminate but quite defiant as well. He had balls. He was happy to say: 'I am who I am.' His hair was quite long, as were his nails, and he sashayed when he walked. His name was Robert. There was another boy called Roland who I always suspected was gay but it was only many years later when I bumped into him in a club that I discovered that he definitely was.

It wasn't so easy for me to get away with it, however. I wasn't allowed to.

There's a particularly memorable line in *The Naked Civil Servant* when Quentin Crisp is sitting in this cafe and a load of ruffians started having a go at him and he said to one of them, 'Why don't you sod off back to Plaistow before I tell them you're queer?' He says at the end of the scene: 'Some queers are really rough, and some roughs are queer.' How true that turned out to be!

The bullying had progressed from name-calling to physical attacks in the showers. I truly hated the showers; they were the scariest and most intimidating experience for me at school. Other boys would whack you with soaking wet towels or stick you under cold water until you screamed for mercy. Every time we had PE I would dart into the showers as fast as I could before they got me. But they regularly did. I was seen as a weakling. They would make a big joke about it. But I also sensed there was something sexual about it.

Looking back on it, I can see now that it was all building up towards some kind of incident. It came one summer when I was fourteen and walking home from school. The teasing and taunting had become so bad that I had started to avoid the main school gate. That's where the bullying was at its worst. Fortunately, I could cut through a wood that led to the school and it didn't take me much longer to get home. I had used this route a few times but one day it proved to be a mistake.

One of the boys who had been trying to intimidate me started following me. He was a big, brutish ugly boy called Alf.

'Here we go again,' I thought. 'He's going to take all my money or try to empty my school bag.' I had got used to that – that had been happening for ages. I'd also been hit a lot.

But, to my surprise, none of these things happened. Instead, he started walking alongside me and began chatting.

It was all fine for a few minutes, but as we passed through a particularly secluded area of the wood, he lurched towards me and pushed me against a tree. He made a clumsy move towards me as if to kiss me. I managed to duck under him and break free, shouting, 'No, no, get off me!'

His reaction was a mixture of embarrassment, anger and a sudden realisation that he had revealed something that could cause him huge problems. He grabbed me again and pinned me back up against the tree. 'If you tell anyone about this, I will kill you,' he said, a kind of terror in his eyes. He then ran off home.

Naively, I dismissed the moment. All I remember thinking was that line from Quentin Crisp and how true it was: 'Some roughs are queer.' But I had underestimated how important that confrontation had been for Alf.

Of course, by the time we went to school the following day he had completely reversed the story and was claiming that I had tried it on with him. And that's when my life became hell. For about the next six months I was pushed and prodded, called every name under the sun. I hated school more than ever – which was quite an achievement.

My one saving grace at school was my friends. Through the paper round that I did, I had become friendly with a couple of lads called Mark and Derek. I'd known them since primary school but it was only now that we had become close. Mark and Derek knew about what had been happening. Neither of them were bothered about the fact that I was a bit effeminate and sensitive. Because they'd known me at primary school, they also knew about my psychic side and what I was capable of doing away from the confines of the classroom and the playground. They were both big and tough enough not to be targets for the bullies. So I began to hang around with them more and more at school. They gave me protection.

My group of friends were more important than ever during this period. In that respect, I guess I was a perfectly normal teenager. I enjoyed nothing more than hanging out with my mates and getting up to normal teenage stuff. The only problem was that in my case, it wasn't remotely normal.

My friends would often ask me to use my psychic abilities to make things happen. I resisted as much as I could; I knew it wasn't something to be taken lightly. But, inevitably, there were times when I gave in. On at least one occasion it landed me in big trouble.

One evening, my mum and dad went out for the night and I invited Mark, Derek and some other friends round to my house. I knew we would have the free run of the place. My grandmother was still living with us but she was getting old and would soon move into a retirement home. My brother was on a sleepover with friends.

There were five of us in all, Derek and Mark, as well as Derek's brother's girlfriend Bev and a girl called Tracy. Maybe it was the presence of the girls, but it put us in high spirits – literally. No sooner did we have the place to ourselves than we were doing what all children of that age do when they are left alone by their parents: we raided my father's drinks cupboard. I can't remember what everyone had but I can recall precisely what I drank. I have to say, to this day I still can't touch Martini Extra Dry – the smell of it alone makes me ill.

It wasn't long before those who had known me from junior school were asking me to perform my 'party piece'. With everyone feeling a little tipsy, Derek turned down the lights and looked at me. 'Shh, everyone, you've got to see this. Colin, do that thing with the lights,' he said.

He and Mark had seen me manipulate the light before and obviously wanted to impress the girls. It wasn't long before I had discovered something that I still preach to this day: disembottled and disembodied spirits don't mix.

I had worked out by now that I wasn't producing effects like the lights or the shaking lampshades on my own. I knew that something else was involved, something that was connected to the spirit world which my grandfather and the old man who sat at the end of the bed inhabited. I knew it was all somehow interconnected. So I had learned that when I wanted to do something like this I had to ask for help. I don't know how I knew this, but I just knew.

I cleared my head as much as I could given the amount of Martini I had drunk and summoned up some help. Everything went as normal at first. I asked for a ball of light to appear and it had soon appeared and begun floating up the wall.

The girls got very excited and there was mixture of cheering and screaming. 'Wow, Colin, how the hell do you do that?' one of them said.

The boys began shouting out instructions: *Make it go there, make it go here.*

Unfortunately, because I'd had a couple of very large glasses of Martini and lemonade and was feeling a bit woozy I couldn't control it. So the light started to dart here, there and everywhere. This only made everyone even more excitable and soon they were all running around the room, trying to catch the dancing ball of light.

It was at this point that Tracy freaked out and ran screaming from the house – much to the amusement of the rest of us who were in fits of laughter. She lived nearby and obviously decided to head home.

We carried on playing around for a little while longer, but pretty soon everyone else was on their way too. I went to bed immediately, feeling a little sick, but unaware that I'd caused any serious problems. My parents got back from their night out none the wiser that we'd had a party. Unfortunately, it didn't stay that way.

The following morning we all got up as usual. My dad headed off to work early leaving me and my mother in the house. We were still eating breakfast when there was a loud 'bang, bang, bang' on the front door. I went to answer it and was soon wishing I hadn't.

Standing there was Tracy and her father, a very stern-looking man, in a suit and tie. He looked like a bank manager. In fact he was a Jehovah's Witness and he was holding a copy of the Bible. I had been completely unaware that Tracy's family were followers. Her father looked really angry and started ranting and raving about me being 'the spawn of the devil' and 'practising the dark arts'.

As he vented his spleen, I hid behind my mother. 'I'm very sorry about this. I can assure you it won't be happening again,' she said, shooting me a glare that could have turned me to stone.

He continued to talk about how 'irresponsible' I had been. He said I was 'dabbling in things that were beyond my comprehension'. He gave a speech that seemed like it was going to go on forever.

To her credit, however, my mother eventually calmed him down and said she'd deal with me. He accepted her apologies and headed off down the road, with a thoroughly miserable-looking Tracy in tow.

My mother was as good as her word. As soon as Tracy and her father had disappeared from view she slammed the front door and hauled me into the kitchen, pulling me by my ear if I remember correctly.

'Right, Colin, what you did was really stupid,' she said, the anger obvious in her voice. 'You have got to start understanding that if you have this ability and you are going to use it, you either do it properly or you don't use it at all.'

I was extremely wary after that and drew a line in the sand with my friends: no more 'party pieces'. As far as my psychic life was concerned, it was kept confined to my home.

The only people I spoke to about what had happened were my mother and Pat. I didn't invite my friends round again for a long time. This meant that I became quite isolated from the rest of the school. I retreated into my shell. And events at home made me even more self-reliant.

My mother had been suffering from back problems for many years, ever since she'd had her accident jumping on the London bus back in her teenage years. At around this time she had another bad fall which required her to be hospitalised. The doctors found that at the point where the spine was buckled before, her latest fall had buckled it the other way.

The end result of this was that my mum had to spend six months in hospital because of the spinal injury. She eventually had a laminectomy, a bone fusion operation, and was – according to our doctors – the first person to have this operation successfully performed. When she came out of hospital she was in a plaster cast, from her chest halfway down one leg.

From my point of view, it meant that once more my mother was absent from my life. I remember the RE teacher at school gave me special dispensation to have Wednesday afternoons off so that I could go to hospital to see her. This meant that I was pretty lonely at home. My dad had all the pressure of trying to keep the family going, while my elderly grandmother ran the home for us. My brother and I weren't that close, and he was only eight in any case. Pat was the only person that I could confide in, but she had four kids to look after and really didn't need a fifth.

In theory it could have been disastrous for me. I could have completely retreated into myself and given up on everything. But, whilst I did become very secretive, my isolation actually made me stronger. Just how strong, I discovered in school one day.

One afternoon I was in a maths class. It was mostly made up of boys and this particularly antagonistic bully was having a go at me as usual. He was coming out with all this homophobic abuse, calling me a poof and a queer. It was a measure of the times that the teacher was ignoring it, which was annoying me enormously. I refused to react so the boy started prodding and pushing me.

For a while now, the anger had been building up inside me. Alone in my room at home, I'd come to a few conclusions about my life. I had decided that I didn't want to be the weakling; I didn't want to be the boy who everyone thought they could push around any longer. That afternoon my temper snapped. It was the first time I'd ever gone into a rage. I had a pair of scissors in my hand for some reason. I sensed my moment and saw that this kid was leaning back in his chair, resting on the desk behind. I jumped up and just pushed him back so that he was arched backwards and pinned down over the desk behind him. I then put the scissors to his throat.

The big kid was panic-stricken. It was so unexpected and so unlike me, I don' t think he had a clue what was going to happen next. To be honest, neither did I.

My actions finally got the teacher's attention. 'Fry, cut it out, stop that,' he said.

A part of me was outraged. I just thought, 'You've been watching this boy verbally and physically abusing me and done nothing about it.' I remember I was shaking with rage. But I knew I had to step back. I had no option. I wasn't going to stab the kid in the throat. I wasn't that crazy.

Unfortunately, this was seen as a sign of weakness by the rest of the class. As I let the big kid loose and returned to my seat they started laughing at me. But I knew a lot of these boys well from the showers and elsewhere. I knew a couple of them had done things that suggested to me they were unsure of their sexuality themselves. I decided to use that against them.

I stood my ground and raised my voice to the rest of the class, ignoring the frankly pathetic teacher who was supposed to be in charge of our welfare. 'If you lot don't start leaving me alone, I'm going to make it public knowledge every person who has ever tried it on with me,' I said.

The effect was instantaneous. Total silence. You could have heard the proverbial pin drop. A lot of the boys were just staring at the floor, terrified of looking up and catching my eye in case anyone else in the class noticed. I felt about six feet tall.

I walked out of that classroom that day and made a promise to myself. 'I will be exactly what they say I am and I will be defiant about it.' I felt a little like Quentin Crisp, if truth be told. It felt like a triumphant moment in my life.

The incident made me feel a lot more secure within myself. I knew I could stand up to the bullies if necessary. But it didn't mean that I enjoyed school any more. In fact, any thoughts I might have had about continuing with school to do O and A levels were quickly disappearing. The straw that broke the camel's back came when I was fourteen or so.

There were two subjects that I really enjoyed: drama and English literature. This was because I had a great English teacher called John Poulson. He got us to read things like *Beowulf* and *The Nun's Priest's Tale* by Chaucer, *The Devil's Disciple* by George Bernard Shaw, and Shakespeare's *The Merchant of Venice*. He was one of the best teachers I had had since Miss Balls at junior school. He taught me how to understand Shakespeare and Chaucer. He just gave me a lifelong passion for literature.

I had also shown a lot of promise in the drama

department. And I had joined a local amateur dramatics group in Haywards Heath, which I loved. At the suggestion of someone connected to the group, my mum and dad enquired on my behalf about a place at the famous Italia Conti drama school. I was really keen on it and pestered them into it. I did an audition, although I can't for the life of me remember where it was or what I performed, but to my amazement and complete joy, I was offered a scholarship. For the first few days after we received the offer I was on cloud nine. All sorts of ideas and thoughts passed through my head. I saw myself on the West End stage, on television, in Hollywood . . . the lot. Well, a boy is allowed to dream. I assumed that accepting the place would be a formality; however, it wasn't that simple. My dreams were quickly crushed.

My parents contacted the school and told them they wanted me to transfer to the Italia Conti. Unfortunately, this had to be approved by the head-master and he called my parents in for a meeting about it. I wasn't there; I wasn't considered important enough, clearly. The headmaster told them that he thought it was a bad idea. In his opinion, there were too few opportunities in the acting profession. I would be far better off staying on at his school, doing my O levels – and maybe even A levels – and getting the qualifications I needed to land 'a proper job'.

My parents were pretty liberal, in general. But when it came to authority they were very old-fashioned. They tended to listen to what people in positions of authority said. And that's what my father did in this instance.

I was absolutely furious. I was also shocked because it mirrored something that I knew he had been through himself. He had been a very talented artist when he was young and had an opportunity to get somewhere with it. But it was blocked by his father, who had, of course, been a frustrated musician too. Instead his father had somehow persuaded him that he should concentrate on getting 'a proper job', whatever that was. I knew it was something that niggled away at him, that nagging question 'what might have been?' I had hoped that he might give me the opportunity that had been denied to him. But he didn't.

I pleaded with my mother in particular, but my father was adamant that it was a firm 'no'. And when my dad said no it always meant no.

Amid the tears and anger that followed, I felt a mixture of emotions. But I also made some firm decisions about the way things were going to be in the future. Firstly, my parents weren't going to be able to keep me in a straitjacket forever. There were things that I could explore without their knowing about it – in particular, when it came to my sexuality and my interest in the psychic world. And secondly, I was absolutely finished with school.

*

For the next two years I paid hardly any attention to my studies, and concentrated instead on being as different to everyone else as humanly possible. By now we were in the late 1970s. It was the time of punk rock. I was good friends with a couple of girls, Yolanda and Maxine, two of the more outrageous pupils at the school. I used to do a typing and commerce class with them, where I was the only boy in the class. They were such a laugh that I became really good friends with them and started dressing in a punky way. I had short spiky hair and began painting my fingernails. How my parents didn't realise I was gay at that point I had no idea.

Our typing teacher was called Mrs Wild. She was very short and used to sit in front of the class. One day Yolanda, Maxine and I decided we'd paint our nails with Tippex, which we thought was hysterically funny. We were also smoking, which we somehow got away with.

As we larked about at the back of the class, some nail varnish remover spilled on to a desk. Somehow a cigarette butt fell into it and it started burning. Before we knew it, the whole bloody desk was in flames. The Formica desk tops started bubbling as the flames grew. Soon we were panicking and shouting and trying to put the flames out with our exercise books. It was only when the screams got completely out of hand that Mrs Wild started shouting at us, 'What are you trying to do, why are you making all those stupid noises?'

It was at that point I suppose that I started to become troublesome. I had always been a fairly well behaved boy. But I was now at the point where I wanted it to be known that I was the square peg that was not going to be fitted into a round hole. I don't think they knew what to do with me. I wasn't deliberately disruptive – I just wouldn't conform.

Having been denied the chance to go to drama school, I also decided to take the plunge and explore my psychic abilities properly. I knew I had some kind of talent, some kind of gift. I wanted to know more about it – and how to use it properly. I no longer wanted to simply send a ball of light bouncing around a room, or make a lampshade move. I wanted more of the kind of experiences I'd had with Miss Walmsley at school.

And so it was one Sunday when I was fifteen that I headed down to Brighton on a train and made my way to one of the Spiritualist churches that Pat had told me about. It was a moment that changed my life.

I had been given the address of the Brighton and Hove Spiritualist Church on Norfolk Terrace. When I got there the church was actually more like a house. There were a few people filing in. When I got to the door I was told that under-eighteens had to be accompanied by an adult. I have always had the ability to think fairly quickly on my feet. 'I'm with that lady inside there,' I said, pointing through the open door at a lady in a bright red hat who was sitting waiting for the service to begin. Somehow they swallowed it and I was allowed in. I still don't quite know how I got away with that.

I'd been to church as a young boy, but this was a very different kind of service. Midway through, after a few hymns, a middle-aged lady appeared at the front of the congregation and began addressing the audience. I was riveted immediately.

She then began passing on messages, seemingly from the dead and departed.

'This must be what Pat and that lady with the crocodile handbag were talking about,' I said to myself. I leaned forward in my chair, desperate to hear every fascinating word.

The lady spoke in a very clear and clipped voice and was very precise in what she said to those who seemed to be receiving messages. They all seemed to mean something to the recipients, but one message in particular stuck in my mind.

At one point, the lady approached a younger woman, who was sitting a couple of rows in front of me. She began to reel off a list of facts about her. 'You are on holiday here in Brighton and you've never been to a Spiritualist church or been to see a medium in your life,' she said.

The woman sat still, neither nodding or shaking her head.

'You've come away to recover from the death of your husband Samuel,' she went on.

Again, the woman sat still.

'Your husband wants you to know that he has influenced you to come here. You have come here from Cape Town with your youngest son, Samuel, but your eldest son, Thomas, was unable to come because he is currently at university in Durban,' she went on.

I was sitting there thinking, 'Where on earth is this lady getting this stuff from?' It seemed incredible to me. Could it all be true?

When the service drew to a close the congregation started drifting away. I was fascinated to know what the woman who'd received the message from her husband had thought.

'I hope you don't mind me asking, but did what the lady said make sense?' I said.

She just nodded and smiled. 'Yes, it did,' she said. She then went on to tell me that it was exactly as the lady had described. 'She was absolutely right about everything. I was just walking past and saw the sign saying Spiritualist Church and thought I have to come in,' she said. She also confirmed that her husband had died recently and that her two sons were in different parts of the world, one here in the UK and the other back in South Africa.

As if the reading hadn't been impressive enough, what was even more amazing was the impact the service had had on this lady. Rather than seeming shocked or upset by what she had heard, she seemed serene. I sensed that somehow she'd needed to hear that message. It was as if a huge weight had been lifted off her shoulders.

It was a profound moment for me: I really felt like a light had been shone into my life. Suddenly the pieces in the puzzling jigsaw that was my teenage life made a little more sense to me. This was the gift that I had been given. Perhaps this is what I should be doing with my own life. For every answer there was another question, of course. How could I learn to harness my talents properly? How could I get to the point where I could practise in a place like this? And how on earth could I get to be as good as the amazing lady I'd seen today?

I returned to the Spiritualist church in Brighton again a couple of weeks later. Once more I had to pretend that I was running late and was going to meet an over-18 inside, and once more the ruse worked. This time I arrived early and spent a few minutes talking to people and reading some of the literature.

I knew already that the Spiritualist Church was a relatively new institution which had taken root in Britain in the mid-nineteenth century. I learned that this particular branch had moved around the town quite a lot and had once occupied a 450-seat venue in the Athenaeum on North Street. I also learned that it had been the venue for a lot of very well known mediums, including a famous man called Maurice Barbanell, whom I'd read about. As well as being the editor of *Psychic News* in the mid part of the twentieth century, Barbanell communicated with a highly evolved spirit called Silver Birch. I knew that his teachings were regarded as being extremely important, in particular in explaining how the hierarchy of the spirit world worked. I felt a real thrill when someone told me that Barbanell had demonstrated for the church in Brighton back in 1926. Another very famous medium whom I'd read about, Ursula Roberts, had also demonstrated there.

So I knew I was in the right place. The service that week didn't contain a reading quite as remarkable as the one I'd witnessed the first time, but it was still fascinating. There was something liberating and at the same time life-enhancing about being in this church. In simple terms, it made me feel good.

I was getting ready to leave at the end of the service when I felt a tap on the shoulder and heard the voice of a lady. 'Hello, young man, what brings you here? I didn't think chaps your age had any time for this sort of stuff,' she said. Before I could say anything I realised who I was talking to: it was the lady who had given the amazing reading to the woman from South Africa the first time I'd attended.

We chatted for a few minutes, during which time I found myself revealing almost everything about myself. I told her about some of the experiences I'd had, from the incident with the Ouija board, to the tarot cards, all the way through to the message I'd passed on to my French teacher.

She looked at me very thoughtfully, as if she was weighing me up. 'Sounds like you should come along to one of my evenings,' she said. She gave me a slip of paper with an address and invited me to come along one Tuesday evening. 'My name's Ida, by the way, what's yours?' she said.

'Colin,' I said, before promising I'd visit her and then heading out the door.

As I made my way home, I could already feel the courage draining from me.

School continued to be largely a waste of time for me. Even my friends were somehow less interesting than the things I was discovering outside the school gates.

The only saving grace was that, as we headed towards the summer exams, we were allowed to read when we had free lessons. So I spent most of the days reading under a tree in a corner of the grounds. But I didn't dare bring any psychic books into the school. That would only be asking for trouble. And I couldn't be bothered studying for any of my exams. So I just read whatever interested me, whether it was books about birds, theatre or – an early passion of mine – antiques. Even when I was a small boy I was strangely drawn to antiques. I still have this love of antique furniture, classical design, antique objets d'art, pocket watches and clocks. I've always been fascinated by old things.

Looking back on it now, I think it was somehow connected to this interest I was forming in lives that had been lived. To be a truly successful medium it's not just about having the ability; it's also about having the compassion and the humility to help people. To have that compassion you have to be interested in the lives of people who have loved. There's a bit of sociology and psychology. You have to be interested in all the things that make a life.

I couldn't have articulated all that back then, of course. The pieces in the jigsaw hadn't even begun to fall into place. And I had no idea what I wanted to be when I left school. I had very strong ideas on what I did NOT want to be, however.

Around this time, we were all expected to go and talk to a careers advice teacher at some point. I was still angry at not having been allowed to go to Italia Conti, so when the teacher asked me what I wanted to do as a job I told him I wanted to be an actor.

'That's a tough one,' he said. 'What else?'

'A chef,' I said.

'Hmm. OK,' he said, making a note.

He then put three leaflets in front of me for the Army, the Navy and the Air Force.

'Why don't you take a look at these and see which one appeals the most. Every boy wants to be in the Forces,' he said.

My response was instant. 'Well not this boy,' I said.

As summer arrived it was time for me to take my exams. I had been entered for a few GCSEs but I had done very little studying. I'd had to take a few mock exams which I'd scraped through partly because I knew a lot of things instinctively – and partly because I cheated. Well, sort of . . .

I had decided I would try to use my psychic abilities to get through a geography exam. When I'd sat down and looked at the paper, I'd realised I knew nothing. The geography teacher was a real dragon and was going to give me hell if I didn't at least attempt to answer the questions. So I did what I did when I wanted a ball of light to appear or the lampshades to move: I asked for help. And it came almost immediately. When I looked down, all the answers started filling themselves in in front of me. I managed to pass the paper. Afterwards the geography teacher said to me, 'I know you cheated, I just don't know how you've done it.'

Many years later she came to one of my demonstrations and came to see me afterwards. 'Now I know how you did it,' she smiled.

Now, of course, some people might wonder why I didn't use my skills like this all the time. The truth was that I had absolutely no interest in passing exams. Somehow I already knew that I was going to succeed in life without these pieces of paper that people kept telling me I needed.

Of course, I was a stubborn teenager and there was an element of defiance in this attitude. But it was also true. I knew for sure that they weren't necessary to get a job. I already had one of those, thanks to my mum, who had got me a job working three nights a week as a waiter in a local restaurant. But I also knew that school wasn't going to teach me what I needed to know. I was going to get that education elsewhere.

As I walked down the street towards the address written on the slip of paper I'd been given at the Spiritualist church a few weeks earlier, my heart was thumping. 'What on earth am I letting myself in for?' I wondered.

By then I'd decided that school was so pointless I couldn't even be bothered to go in any more. Instead, I'd told myself that visiting the medium I'd met in Brighton, Ida, was a much more constructive way of spending my time. There was nothing to lose, was there? The sparks of courage I'd summoned up to get myself to the railway station and onto the train to Brighton were slowly ebbing away.

However, Ida greeted me with a warm smile and invited me into a small dining room that seemed to be full of other people. In fact there were a dozen of us in there. She went around the table introducing everybody. Most of the people were young, although none of them was quite as young as me. I was certainly the only schoolboy there.

Ida was a very straightforward, plain-speaking woman who made her feelings clear from the beginning. She let us know in no uncertain terms that becoming a medium wasn't easy. It was extremely hard work, and would be too much for most of us. 'There are twelve of you here tonight. Within three weeks, six of you will have gone and six will remain,' she said.

Then she went on to say something that sent a shiver down my spine: 'Of the six who stay, two will go on to become working mediums, what I call "workers". But only one of those two will have a career in it. The other one will pass over at an early age.' There was a deathly silence when she said this. I could feel everyone looking at each other.

Once we'd recovered from Ida's slightly scary speech, the evening was really interesting and enjoyable. The main part involved us all sitting around a table in a circle with the lights dimmed. Ida began by channelling a message to one of the regular members. It was actually intended for a friend of hers who was having marital difficulties, but she said she would pass it on.

After that two of the other group members attempted to communicate what they were picking up on. It was clear that they were apprentices whereas Ida was an expert.

As I chatted to the others over a cup of tea afterwards, I learned that she could well have become a professional. At the time the most prominent mediums in Britain were Doris Stokes and Doris Collins. 'Ida could have been as big as them, easily,' the oldest and most experienced of the other people there told me. 'She has been asked to demonstrate all over the world. But she's not interested in performing in theatres and staying in a different hotel every night. That's not why she is doing it,' he said.

I left mightily relieved that I'd come through it without making a fool of myself. I resolved to go back every week. I felt like I had taken an important step.

I went back to Ida the following week and enjoyed myself even more. By now I'd also been to another Spiritualist church in Brighton, just to get a feel for the different styles. To my surprise, Ida had been there as well. It turned out she was a regular at many local churches and was always in demand as a medium.

I learned so much from her, not just practical things, but in general. She helped me understand the 'big picture' about the spirit world even though I'd read a lot by this point. I'd devoured books on subjects like astral projection and Spiritualist societies. I'd read a book about Kathryn, a contemporary trance medium controlled by White Hawk, a Native American. My reading was beginning to open up doors that explained the sorts of things that had happened to me during my childhood. It was all beginning to make a kind of sense.

But being a student of Ida's was very tough-going. She was very strict. She was going to be a hard taskmaster, I could tell that already. When I'd seen her at work in the Spiritualist church I'd noticed how detailed and accurate she was. She demanded the same from her students. She would always push us to give details, because details are what people want.

She explained that, as a medium, you are bombarded with a mass of information. It is as if the whole of the afterlife is speaking to you at once. She used to say that the spirit world is projecting out 1,000 thoughts at you at 100 miles per hour. The role of the medium was to capture as many of those thoughts as possible. She said that if you don't try and focus you will only pick up two or three, but if you do try and you train and develop yourself then you should be able to pick up hundreds of those thoughts. She made no bones about the fact that it wasn't easy. She used to say that the best medium in the world will never pick up everything that is transmitted. But we had to try. That was our job: to capture as many of these thoughts as possible and then to distil them down and communicate them to others.

Every session with her was fascinating. She taught us about the levels of existence and about how the spirit world is a vibration of ether, not matter, and how it therefore resonates at a faster rate. She was an amazing teacher. I learned so much every time I went to visit her. It was a revelation to me.

One morning in July 1976 I put on my school uniform, slung my satchel over my shoulder and headed to school for the very last time. It was a day I had been looking forward to with relish. By now my hatred for

the place had reached an all-time high. I'd clearly sig-
nalled to the teachers that I couldn't give a stuff. I had
sat a few GCSEs but knew that I wouldn't scrape a pass
in any of them. I wasn't even sure I'd check the results
when they came out during the summer.

I knew I was leaving and that my education was
going to continue in a very different sphere. I'm sure
my disdain was written all over my face. Inside I was
thinking, how could school teach me that I was going
to become a medium? It couldn't, it didn't have the
capacity to do that. I was never going to fit into a
conventional mould.

There had, of course, been some happy moments.
And I had met some great teachers. But the entire
experience was summed up for me on that last day by
the attitude of the staff. There were a lot of very reac-
tionary, right-wing bullies there, most of them men.
One of them, a big, beer-bellied teacher, who'd been
there for years, was particularly unpleasant.

I was walking down a corridor on my own when
he saw me.

'Last day today, isn't it, Fry?' he said.

'That's right, sir,' I said.

'Any idea what you are going to do?'

'Oh, I'm not sure, sir. I'm sure something will show
up,' I said, slightly cockily.

I knew he didn't like me and I knew that in particular he didn't like the fact that I was so effeminate.

'Yes, I'm sure it will, Fry. I hear the council are

looking for dustmen.' It wasn't a joke. It was just a nasty, snide remark. And it was typical of him and, I am afraid to say, the school.

Many years later, when I started appearing on television, the secretary of the school contacted me to ask if I would come back to open the Christmas Fete. I told them that I would rather stick blunt needles in my eyes than go back to that place.

I was the square peg that they tried to fit in the round hole – and they had failed.

That afternoon I walked out of the school gates and down the road towards home feeling on top of the world. I was so glad to be out of that place that I pulled out a cigarette lighter and set fire to my tie. (Much to my mother's annoyance because my brother was starting the same school a year later and she wanted the tie for him.)

I remember so clearly thinking at the time: *no one will ever put me down again and I am going to do and be whatever I want to be in life.*

6 | Guiding Spirits

I LEFT school without any qualifications or a place at college. But as far as I was concerned I was now heading off to the University of Life, a place that was going to be of far more use to me than any academic institution.

The first thing I needed to do was to get a job. That had never been much of a problem for me. I'd had a string of part-time jobs while I was at school and wasn't afraid of hard work. Pretty quickly I landed myself a great job, working as a commis chef at a restaurant called the Bolney Stage. I'd worked in various restaurants with my mother, doing stints as a waiter and even as a dishwasher in a teahouse in Lindfield. But my mother was keen that I learn to be a proper chef. I wouldn't do any real cooking as a commis chef, just a lot of chopping up vegetables, preparing salads and food for the head chef, a fun Irishman called – I kid you not – Frank Carson. But it was a first step on the ladder.

I enjoyed it, far more than I had enjoyed school – that was for certain. I threw myself into it enthusiastically, to the point where I got told off by Frank for mopping the kitchen floor while the place was empty. 'That's someone else's job,' he'd growled at me.

Things were going so well that they had suggested I start a day-release course at a local catering college. But it was not to be. Unfortunately, three months into the job I developed dermatitis on my hand, which was obviously a huge problem given that I was working in a very hygienic environment. Yet in a way it was a godsend. The job was already interfering with my psychic development because I had to work split shifts. I would often have to work Sundays, for instance, which meant I couldn't go to the Spiritualist churches. Evening development circles and visits to Ida in Brighton were also inconvenient.

I was disappointed but not devastated to leave. It didn't take me long to get another job, this time working in a carpet shop run by two brilliant guys, Brian Ashard and Eric Stone, and their four sons. Their chain had four or five branches across the Sussex area. I was given the job of junior salesman in the Burgess Hill branch. I really enjoyed every aspect of it.

I was also expanding my horizons in other ways. Around my sixteenth birthday I had discovered this huge – but then underground – gay community in Brighton. Looking back on it now, I wondered how people knew it even existed. One Saturday, I'd put on my most adult clothes and headed into Brighton in search of it. One of the things that I quickly discovered about the gay community then was that it was very insular and very protective of its own. There was a real hierarchy with these 'old queens' who made sure they looked after the younger gays. I, of course, fell very firmly into the latter camp.

At that time the 'queen mother' of Brighton was an older guy called Keith. Everyone used to call him just that, Mother. If older men would ply us with drinks or try to take advantage, Keith or one of his cohorts would step in and warn them off.

I wasn't the only young guy finding his way into this community; there was another chap called Terry. He was a bit more familiar with the gay scene and we became friends. He and I used to go to a pub called The Spotted Dog, where they were a bit more lenient about under-age drinkers. It was quite obvious we were under age, of course. I remember once the landlord said to me: 'I know you are bloody under age, so if the police ever come in you come and hide under the counter here.'

I was barely out of school, so I continued to conceal my emerging sexuality from my parents. At this point, I was still living at home and I behaved very differently there. I always made sure I was back to looking normal by the time I got home. You've got to remember the times. It was 1976 or so. Even then I was 'the only gay in the village'. People forget how much things have changed.

Today, of course, I wouldn't have bothered hiding anything. But I always knew that my father would have a problem coping with it. My mother had her suspicions, of course.

When I was fifteen she had asked me outright, 'Are you gay?' But at the time I hadn't felt confident enough to tell the truth.

So for a while I'd pretended to have a couple of girlfriends. One was called Samantha, or Sam, the other Tracy. We were actually close friends and did hang out together, even going to the cinema. But as relationships they weren't going to go anywhere. For me it was convenient. It was a bit unfair on the girls because they were probably more interested in me than I was in them. Of course, there's a little part of me that was probably thinking maybe I will become heterosexual.

My sexuality was becoming more and more of an issue for me. I had effectively 'come out' at school and had begun living the life of a young gay man in Brighton. It was a dangerous path to take in many ways, as I would eventually discover.

Work and the gay scene were two parts of my education in life. The third, and most important part, was being provided by Ida and my work at the Spiritualist Church.

At that point in my development as a psychic, I wasn't lacking in confidence. It was only strengthened by events around this time, in particular one very unexpected encounter.

One day, while I was down in Brighton, I was talking to a friend who worked at the Dome. He knew I was interested in spiritualism and mediumship. 'Colin, did you know Doris Stokes is coming to the Dome next month?' he said. 'If you fancy coming along I can get you a cheap ticket. I might even be able to get you backstage so you can meet her.'

'Really?' I said, excited. 'That would be incredible.'

I asked a couple of people at Ida's group whether they wanted to join me and, a few weeks later, we went along to the Dome for the show. It was a truly memorable evening, not just because I got a chance to glimpse the woman who was without question the most entertaining and insightful medium I ever saw demonstrating publicly. When the demonstration was over my friend was good to his word and ushered me and one of my friends backstage. The others were a bit too star-struck and decided to wait in the foyer.

We met Doris's husband John first. He was incredibly friendly. He then led us to Doris's dressing room. She was having a cup of tea but waved us in. The minute we stepped into the small, cramped room she came over to me, ignoring my friend. I will never, ever forget what she said. 'Oh hello, dear,' she said. 'My guide is telling me that you've got the gift.'

I knew from the books and articles I'd read that Doris had a famous spirit guide called Romanoff so I worked out later that it must be him. At the time, I was too flabbergasted to think anything. Doris went on to tell me that I was going to be a world-famous medium, that I would find global fame in my fortieth year and that I was going to travel the world demonstrating. She was even specific about where I was going to go, mentioning Australia, New Zealand and even Japan.

To be honest, I couldn't take it seriously. As if sensing this, Doris then told me that she could see a man with a bad back and a shadow over his eye standing behind me. That got my attention. I realised immediately that it was my grandfather Lawrie. She then seemed to have a brief conversation with him, smiling when he told her that he had been at my side ever since he had passed over. 'That's nice,' she said.

We were only in the room for a few minutes, but in that brief time she had blown me away. I couldn't stop talking about it with my friends for days afterwards. It made a permanent impression on me. For years a part of me had wondered whether I had been imagining seeing my grandfather, whether I had somehow wished him back into existence because I missed him so much. Any doubts I had that I had really been visited by his spirit were dispelled that night in Doris Stokes' dressing room.

That meant that the old man I regularly saw was also real, as were the spirit children, like the little curly-haired boy John, who was tugging at his mother's coat as his mother drank tea with mine all those years ago. Suddenly a giant piece in the confusing jigsaw that was the whole psychic world slotted into place for me.

In the days that followed, I also wondered about what Doris had said to me, about me travelling the world doing what she did in far-flung countries. Surely that couldn't be true? Could it?

In the weeks and months that followed that night I flung myself into my training with Ida. I read and studied as much new material as I could. I knew I had so much to learn. And I was determined to learn it.

I felt like I was already making real progress at Ida's development circle. At first, I'd been content to sit on the sidelines, observing what was going on. But Ida had quickly thrown me into the deep end, pushing me to explore my abilities. She seemed to have faith in me, but there were also fewer of us there. As Ida had predicted, half of the dozen who had originally started with the circle had disappeared within three weeks. Of the remaining six, two of us, myself and a guy called Mark, seemed to be the ones with the most natural aptitude. (Tragically, Ida's other prediction came right and, a few years later, he died at the far-too-early age of just twenty-seven.)

One evening we arrived, as usual, to find one or two unfamiliar faces there. One of them was a woman who had come along as a guest. She was quite an attractive lady, nicely dressed. When she said 'good evening' to everyone I detected a mild American accent. She seemed old to me then, but I was only seventeen. Thinking back, she was probably only in her early forties.

'Would you mind being a test subject?' Ida asked the lady as we settled down to get the evening under way.

'No, not at all,' she replied, sitting back in her chair as if not sure what to expect next.

Moments later, after making her usual brief introduction, Ida turned to me. 'Colin, can you please tell this lady what you sense,' she said, looking at the American visitor.

I was caught off guard a bit by this, but it didn't take me long to compose myself. As I concentrated I found myself making a very strong connection. 'There is a very well proportioned black man standing right behind you,' I said to the lady.

Almost immediately Ida interjected. She had a very strong rule that we did not mention people's 'spirit guides', the guardian angels that watch over many of us, especially those with psychic abilities.

'No, no, no, Colin. You know we don't do guides,' she said, impatiently.

'No, it's not her guide,' I said. 'It's someone else, I'm sure.'

'Hmm,' Ida said, settling back into her chair, before waving with her hand in a signal for me to carry on.

'This man is telling me that his name is Earl,' I said.

At that point the American lady just burst into tears. I felt awful. 'I'm sorry – are you all right?' I said.

'Yes, but you've just described my husband,' she said.

I could feel the others taking a sharp intake of breath. I threw a quick glance at Ida but she just nodded as if to say 'carry on'. She was watching me intently.

'Would you be able to understand that he is telling me you had to move around a lot in the years you were together and although you loved each other a lot, your marriage was never easy,' I said.

She nodded and said, 'Yes.'

'He has just shown me a date, the first of July, and he is telling me it has two meanings,' I said. 'Does that mean anything to you?'

'Yes, it does.'

'Ah, I see,' I then said, as the message revealed itself in all its clarity. 'He was born on the first of July and he died on the same day.'

'Yes, that's right, he died on his birthday,' she said, dabbing at her eyes with a handkerchief.

'He was only thirty-six years of age when he died,' I said.

'Yes, that's correct.'

The connection faded soon after that, but not before Early Earl had passed on his love to his wife. When I turned to Ida, she had an approving look on her face, although she didn't say anything more than 'thank you, Colin' at that point.

It was an experience the likes of which I'd not had before. I'd seen and heard spirits and passed on messages before, but not in such a pressurised situation and in such detail.

Afterwards, the rest of the group took it in turns to pass on messages, some of them again using the American lady as their 'test subject'. But they weren't able to get anything more than some uninspiring messages about sensing her mother and seeing lots of white flowers. As each one finished, Ida said 'thank you' but it was clear that she wasn't particularly impressed, even with Mark, on this particular occasion.

As the circle broke up and we all gathered our coats ready to leave, Ida asked me to wait for a second. 'Could I have a quick word with you, Colin,' she said.

She made me a cup of tea and sat me down. 'You really are getting very, very good. You were very impressive tonight,' she said.

I was elated. I knew how hard it was to please her and hadn't heard her speak in such gushing terms before. It didn't last long, however.

'But you shouldn't let it go to your head,' she said, with an arched eyebrow. 'You're still very young and have got so much to learn. You have got to practise this thing now of getting deeper into the feelings of the person with whom you are connecting,' she said. 'A good medium is someone who can empathise and understand what people are feeling. To be able to do that, you need a few grey hairs.'

This suggestion that I was somehow too young to feel anything was something that I was beginning to resent a little bit. At the Spiritualist church I had heard this a lot. A lot of the older mediums kept saying to me: 'When you are older, you will be quite good.' I always felt a bit patronised by that. Of course, they were right. I just didn't realise it yet. That would soon change, however.

7 | Breaking Point

TODAY I know that Ida was right: to be a successful medium you need to be able to do a lot more than simply receive and relay messages from the spirit world. In order to interpret, translate and communicate the thoughts, feelings and impulses you are picking up you also have to have some experience of life. I'd seen that with Doris Stokes. She had an immense gift for empathising and sympathising with people here in the earthly realm as well as in the spirit world. I'd witnessed it first hand backstage.

As a teenager, I was becoming confident that I had the ability to tap into the spirit world. What I didn't yet understand was that I still needed the life experience to interpret it all properly. That all changed in the space of the next couple of years, however. I went through what you might call a crash course in life experience. I was lucky to come out alive.

Being overtly gay back then was a perilous thing to do. There was a lot of homophobia around, but there were also a lot of people who were suppressing their sexuality. Some of them were predatory. I don't want to go into great detail about it, but around this time I was the victim of rape.

As with so many crimes, it happened close to home.

One weekend I went to visit a girl friend of mine at her parents' house. I arrived there to discover her father was in the house on his own. He explained that his wife and daughters were out shopping, but would be back soon. He then asked me if I wanted a cup of tea. I said yes, not thinking there was anything abnormal going on at all. I knew the man and the family reasonably well. He was a local shopkeeper in my home town.

It all happened in a blur. He attacked me and, despite my best efforts, I was completely powerless to stop him. He was average build, but he was stronger than me.

I said nothing to anyone at the time; it took me many years to talk about it. I just avoided him and the family. It was only many years later when I was working as a floor manager in a department store in Haywards Heath that I saw him again. He came in with his wife to buy a carpet and I had to serve him. It was at that point I thought, 'The shame is yours, not mine.' I made a decision not to say anything.

He died of a heart attack in his early fifties. I vowed then that I would never reveal who he was. The two girls didn't deserve to have the memory of their father destroyed. By that time I had learned to live with what he did to me.

My feeling at the time, however, was very different. My first instinct was to blame myself. They say a lot of rape victims persuade themselves that they had somehow 'asked for it'. That was how I felt for a while. I believed I must have given some indication or some signal, he must have thought that was what I wanted.

But strangely almost immediately it made me stronger. I had only recently overcome the bullying at school, so I drew on the same reserves of strength that I'd used there. I put the two things together and I made a decision.

This thing had happened, and I wished it hadn't. But it had taught me that I wasn't going to be used by anyone again.

There's no doubt that the experience threw me into a spin for a while. Its repercussions were immense, and continued to affect me for a long time afterwards in ways I didn't really understand until many years later. In the short term, I lost my bearings for a while, making some bad decisions, the worst of which was to move to London, of all places.

I don't quite know where the idea came from. Perhaps I was running away from Sussex after what happened to me. Perhaps I was running away from a small community so that I could lose myself in the faceless masses of London. I quit my job at the carpet shop in Burgess Hill and got a job at another carpet shop, in East Sheen, southwest London. I found myself some cheap lodgings in Isleworth and started what I thought was going to be a new life. I was there for six disastrous months.

Quite simply, I was only seventeen years of age and far too young to be away from home. I didn't know how to look after myself. On top of that, I didn't know that many people either. Finding a gay community like the one in Brighton was pretty much impossible – well, for me anyway. London was so vast and cosmopolitan, I was completely out of my depth and easy prey for those whose intentions were not good to me.

I did have one memorable moment there. At one point I became friendly with a guy who was going through what we would today call a gender reassignment, but back then was known as a sex change. His name was Steve and he was becoming Stella.

He was only a little bit older than me but he seemed much more worldly-wise. He became a good friend, even if he did have a tendency to be a little too outrageous at times.

One day he turned up at my digs in East Sheen to announce that he'd lined up a double date for us, with two sailors from Portsmouth. To my absolute horror, he then announced that they were expecting two girls.

Being young and foolish, I agreed to go along with Steve/Stella's plan and 'dragged up'. He had plenty of women's clothing so I stuffed my bra with cotton wool, shaved what little hair I had on my legs and arms and tottered off to Leicester Square to meet the two sailors. I was absolutely terrified when we met them. They seemed nice enough guys, who took us for a drink then bought us tickets to go see a movie, Stephen King's *Carrie*.

As soon as we got into the cinema they started to get a bit frisky. Steve/Stella didn't mind this at all, but I really wasn't sure. I kept thinking what would happen if this poor, unsuspecting sailor had managed to get his hand inside my bra. I endured two hours of the film but as soon as the house lights came up at the end I dragged Steve/Stella off to the toilets – the ladies', naturally.

'Right, this has gone on long enough. We've got to run for it,' I said.

I can only imagine the sight we must have made as we ran across Leicester Square screaming for a taxi – and how frustrated the two sailors must have felt wondering where their two very peculiar dates had disappeared to.

Sadly this story has an unhappy footnote. I lost touch with Steve but heard through someone else many years later that he had failed to get the surgery he wanted in this country and had headed to Brazil to have the procedure done there. He died on the operating table. I still think of him as someone who taught me not to judge someone because they are different.

Nevertheless, that evening was a rare highlight in a pretty awful period in my life. I quickly realised that I'd made a terrible mistake. So, within six months of heading off I returned to Sussex with my tail between my legs.

I was incredibly lucky. The carpet shop gave me my old job back: the position hadn't been filled since I'd left. Even better, when I turned eighteen that May, the owners asked me whether I'd like to run a shop on my own. They had a small shop called Rems and Ends in Gardner Street in Brighton and needed someone to look after it. I leapt at the chance. At first I began commuting down there every day from Haywards Heath.

One day, travelling to work I found myself sitting opposite a teacher from my old school. She was actually rather a nice teacher and we got chatting. I told her about what I was doing work-wise. She said something I will never forget: 'I can never tell my pupils this at school, but the fact is that it's not the place for everyone and some people only begin to shine when they leave.' How true that was.

After a while the commuting became a bore and I decided I'd like to move to Brighton. It was at this point that I met two people who would become hugely important in my life, for very different reasons.

I had become very close to Keith, or 'Mother' as we knew him. He was very protective of me and made sure that I didn't fall in with the wrong people. When I went round to his place one day, there was a guy there who was older than me, in his mid thirties. As we got talking, it became apparent that he had been brought up in Haywards Heath and that he knew my mum very well. He and she had been brought up together as kids. I took an instant liking to him. He was very quick and wise and witty. His name was Michael Cotton. He very rapidly became my best friend.

Michael was thirty-five and I was barely eighteen. This was, and would remain, a recurring pattern for me. I have always looked up to older people and drawn on their wisdom. Many of them have inspired me and Michael would certainly do that.

It was also around that time that I met someone who would be my partner for twenty-two years – Chris. He worked in a bar in Brighton and was good-looking and intelligent. He was older than me and more romantic. I still wasn't openly gay. We hit it off and began a proper relationship. He was my first proper boyfriend, effectively.

Of course, being the cusp of the 1970s and 1980s, it wasn't quite as simple as it appeared. I was eighteen and he was twenty-three so our relationship at the time was totally illegal. The age of consent then was twenty-one. So our relationship had to be conducted very carefully.

Fortunately, the gay community were able to help us. My friend Keith, Mother, lived in a big house in one of the gay enclaves, Norfolk Road. He persuaded the landlord to let me have a small bedsit in the same house. My mother and father weren't best pleased that I was moving out again at such a young age, especially after the ill-fated adventure in London. But at that stage in my life I didn't care. I had reached an important crossroads.

It wasn't that I didn't get on with my family, because I did. My mother and I, in particular, were closer in my teens than we'd ever been. I think we understood each other better than we'd ever done. But I felt I had to leave for various reasons.

First, I knew there had to be more to life than Haywards Heath. I'd spent all my life in and around the town. There had to be a bigger world out there and I wanted to experience that bigger world. Second, however, I really needed to be myself. This was a time when people weren't openly gay and I wanted to be openly gay. The only way to do that was to do it within a community that accepted me. And that community was in Brighton. But in addition, I had this special ability that most people didn't understand. I wanted to explore it and to explore my spirituality as well. Brighton was the perfect place to do that, both in church and in Ida's development circles.

For me, the bedsit was absolutely perfect. It was tiny but it meant I could go to the Spiritualist churches at the weekends, and I could live openly in the middle of the gay community.

I was soon revelling in my newfound freedom. Soon after I moved in I got myself a second job, working part-time behind the bar in a gay club, The Palace, under the Palace Hotel. I had just turned eighteen when I got the job. Although the age of consent was twenty-one I was old enough to work in a pub. It meant I was burning the candle at both ends. The Palace had a 2 am licence and by the time I'd cleared up it was sometimes 3 am when I got home. I would then have to be up and out by 8 am to work at the carpet shop. But I was young and able to survive on only a few hours' sleep.

As I began my relationship with Chris, I felt a real mixture of emotions. On the one hand, I felt like I was growing up, becoming an adult. Yet on the other I still felt like I was leading a secret life. My family, in particular, had absolutely no idea of the existence I was leading twenty miles away from Haywards Heath. It didn't sit well with me, and so I decided that I had to come clean, or, more accurately, come out.

Chris worked behind the bar of the Heart & Hand on the seafront in Brighton, near my bedsit. He stayed over one night and I was meeting my mum the following day, Wednesday, my day off. I told him how I felt about this secrecy and somehow convinced myself that I had to spill the beans the following day.

I got up the next morning determined to go through with it. I had the whole speech planned in my head. I met my mum at the railway station and then took her out to lunch. It was like something out of a movie: every time I was close to saying what I wanted to say, something happened. A waiter would arrive, or my mother would want to go and 'powder her nose'. Finally, after about half an hour, I had started forming the words, 'Mum, there's something I need to talk to you about . . .' At that precise moment, two rather camp guys came into the coffee shop.

'Oh, look at the state of those two,' my mum said, a look of disdain on her face.

That was it, I just bottled it. I just thought to myself, 'I can't tell her.' When she asked me what it was that was so important that I wanted to tell her, I made up some story about my flat being cold and wanting to borrow a paraffin heater from home.

I was so upset that night I cried. The frustration was eating away inside me. I was proud of who I was and the life I was leading. I didn't want to keep it a grubby little secret any longer. I barely slept a wink and got up the next morning more resolved than ever to tell my family the truth.

It took me another two days to finally summon the courage, but I did it. I went to the phone booth at the bottom of my road one afternoon and told my mother over the phone. Her reaction was predictable – she was hysterical, absolutely hysterical. She couldn't believe it.

'Mum, there's a lot worse things that could have happened, I haven't changed as a person,' I said.

But she just couldn't comprehend it. It was the most emotional phone call I'd ever made.

Afterwards I met Chris for a coffee and told him what I'd done.

'I bet they turn up at my bedsit tonight,' I said, half joking to Chris.

Sure enough they did. I was just getting ready to go to work at the bar, when they appeared on my doorstep. They were very upset – my father, in particular, looked shaken to the core. He was animated and started talking at me immediately. 'Son, we can sort this out. I will get you a doctor,' he said. 'You are moving back home. You have to get away from this place – it's the influence of all these people around you that's turned you this way.'

I was outraged. 'Dad, I don't need a doctor. This isn't something that has happened recently. It's not someone else's influence, it's me. I've always been like this.'

They left in a fury, swearing that this wasn't the end of the matter and that they'd be back again to 'talk sense into me'.

I was upset and headed to work late. I met up with Chris later and spent most of the night drinking with some other friends. They were a huge help. Most of them had suffered the same problems. 'Oh, my mother understands it but my father doesn't. We just don't talk about it,' one said to me. 'I was thrown out of the house and told never to darken their doorstep again,' another one told me.

In hindsight I can see that I handled it all wrongly. I had made the cardinal error of expecting my parents automatically to accept the fact I was gay. I hadn't taken into account that parents have expectations of their children. For right or wrong, they carry around this subconscious version of life in which their children will do what they did – leave school, get a job, get married and have children. If you suddenly march into breakfast and announce 'guess what?' you can't expect them to immediately and instinctively accept that you are gay. It's not fair on them. They need a period of adjustment, they need to get used to the idea.

So I have always regretted the way I handled my coming out and if I were giving any advice to a young person today, I would say that you have to put a lot of work in to explain to your family that you are different – different but normal.

But I didn't do that. I had been desperately trying to hide it from my parents. They weren't homophobic but they probably did have that idea that it 'wasn't the sort of thing that happens in our family' – even though it must have done, and always had done.

And so it was that I got on with the life of being an openly gay man in Brighton. It seems unbelievable today but we were the outsiders in society back then.

Even the police gave us a hard time and tried to intimidate us. They would raid The Palace club, where I worked in the evenings, on a regular basis – often asking us for our names and addresses, even though there was no legal obligation to give our details to them.

That was the bad news. The good news was that Brighton had a big gay community so there was safety in numbers.

Having broken the news to my parents, I felt I could take the next step and move in with Chris. There was a larger bedsit upstairs in the same building and the landlord was willing to give it to us. For a while, I was blissfully happy. I had what I thought was the ideal existence. I even patched things up with my mother, who returned to her routine of coming down to see me every Wednesday.

Yet my father still wasn't talking to me, of course, and never came to visit. It made life difficult for my brother, who was thirteen by now and who did want to come and see me. But he was conflicted because he knew that our dad would disapprove. Word had got round in our home town that I had come out. I cannot comprehend how difficult that must have made my brother's life. So I bit the bullet and started visiting them. I would head back up for a Sunday lunch or something every now and again, sometimes staying over for the night.

One night I saw my old friend from school, Mark.

We had a drink together and I told him my big news: I was gay.

I don't know what sort of reaction I was expecting, but he just arched an eyebrow and said, 'Colin, tell me something that I didn't already know.' I laughed like a drain.

It wasn't long before things started to go wrong, however. I was besotted with Chris. It was a real 'first love' situation. I wanted to be with him twenty-four hours a day, especially during the summer months when Brighton was at its liveliest. Rather foolishly, I gave up my part-time job at the Palace club, and got a full-time job in the same bar as Chris, my idea being that we could spend all our time together – but that's not really a good idea in any relationship! I also found myself taking less interest in Ida and the Spiritualist church.

She, of course, picked up on this immediately. On the last evening I attended she spoke to me as I was leaving, almost sensing that we wouldn't see each other for a while.

'You are going to go through a very difficult time in your life; it is going to be very painful. But remember when someone has served a purpose in your life you have to let them go,' she said to me as I headed off into the night.

I had no idea what it meant and pretty much dismissed it immediately. For now I'd lost interest in her, in spiritualism and mediumship, in pretty much anything – except for Chris.

Of course, it was a recipe for disaster. Over the course of the next few months my 'dream' new life slowly began turning into a nightmare. The first blow came when the summer season drew to an end and the place went quiet. One night while I was working at the pub the manager pulled me over and told me that they would have to let me go. So I had no job. I worked briefly at a tailoring shop which I hated. For a while I was on the dole.

Things spiralled downhill from there. I had no money and too much time on my hands. Inevitably it affected my relationship with Chris. We began arguing a lot and eventually split up. I was devastated. It had been my first proper relationship and it had failed.

Looking back on it now, I can see that throughout that period I had been bottling up a lot of emotions. In particular, I'd suppressed a lot of my anger and upset at being attacked by a friend's father. My break-up with Chris was the straw that broke the camel's back. Suddenly the floodgates opened. I had what today we'd call a mini-breakdown.

I felt absolutely shattered. I'd given up a job that I'd loved, split up with my boyfriend and cut myself off from my family. Spiritualism and my interest in mediumship had fallen by the wayside as well. I really felt like I'd mucked up my life. It was around September or October 1981. I was a complete mess.

One evening, I went into the bathroom of my bedsit, opened the small cabinet above the sink and pulled out a packet of paracetamol and a shaving razor. I poured myself a glass of water and hurled down what must have been a dozen tablets. I then removed the blade from the razor and dug it into my wrists, first the left then the right.

It was stupidity, teenage stupidity. For a minute or two I sat there, with my arms over the sink, blood flowing out. It didn't take long for me to see sense. I don't remember hearing any voices or feeling the presence of anyone, but I have a feeling that perhaps the spirit world might have played its part.

I was still conscious, mainly because, as I could see, I hadn't managed to cut very deep at all with the blade. It was deep enough to leave a scar, one I have to this day. But it probably wasn't terminal. I realised what I'd done and how stupid I'd been. I wrapped my arms up in tea towels, got myself into a taxi and drove off to the hospital. I arrived in the Accident and Emergency Department at around 9 pm.

I just walked up to the main reception desk, held out my hands with the blood-soaked tea-towels around them and said, 'I've done something really stupid.' Of course, a part of me was screaming out for attention, for someone to put their arm around me and comfort me. I didn't get it. Instead a male nurse appeared, took a quick look at me and came to the conclusion that it wasn't life-threatening. 'You'll live, take a seat over there until you are called to see a nurse,' he said, turning on his heels and heading off to deal with someone a little bit more deserving of his medical care.

For the next half an hour or so I sat there, alone with my thoughts. I really had been an idiot. What on earth had I been thinking? What was I hoping to achieve?

Eventually I was seen by a young, male doctor. There was also a nurse in attendance. They were a little bit more sympathetic. After they'd made me drink a pint of salt water so that I vomited up the tablets, they asked me a series of questions. 'How old are you?' the doctor asked as they finished off the bandaging.

'Nineteen,' I mumbled.

'Take my advice and go home.'

Before I could leave I had to fill in some paperwork. They asked me who to notify. I said my parents.

Of course, my mother and father were horrified. They headed down immediately and this time I agreed to go home with them.

They were sympathetic at first, and there was no doubt that my father was delighted to get me home, and away the 'den of iniquity' that was Brighton.

But it wasn't long before they made their real feelings plain. The next day I had a huge row with my mother. 'What the hell were you thinking?' she shouted at me. 'If you were feeling so depressed or unhappy, why on earth didn't you come and see us?'

At one point, my father's eldest brother Dave turned up. He was always a cool head in a crisis and had been instrumental in trying to get my dad to accept me being gay. I learned later that he'd warned my dad that if he didn't change his attitude towards me then he risked losing me, which was true.

My mother told Dave to come and have a word with me. He found this sobbing prima donna lying on his bed. He was as forthright with me as he had been with my father. Dave told me to get a grip on myself. 'You might be different. But you've got to lead a normal life.'

He was dead right, of course.

The person who helped me most during this phase, however, was undoubtedly Michael. In the weeks that followed my suicide attempt he came to see me regularly. He was a real shoulder to cry on. Because he'd known my mother for a long time, he was always welcome around our house. And because he was an older, more mature man, he had befriended my dad as well. My father knew Michael was gay, but he understood that he was a good influence on me.

I think my parents were sympathetic to him also because Michael had no family. He had been raised in a Barnardo's home as a kid and had never known any relatives.

So he started spending more and more time with us, including Christmases. He became almost a member of the family.

As I tried to get myself together, Michael's advice to me was invaluable. He kept telling me that what was happening to me was just a phase I was going through. 'Things are going to get better, you will get back on your feet. You're only nineteen, this is just a blip,' he would say. And he was right, of course. It was just that, a blip.

Getting myself back on my two feet wasn't that easy, however. The only work I could get was a part-time job, cleaning classrooms at a private school in Ardingly. I hated it and the pay was terrible, but it did help get me back on track. I had soon got another job. My mum became a house mother at a school for emotionally and educationally disturbed children. One day she came home from work and told me that they needed an assistant cook. I went for the job and got it. I didn't exactly have the best of relationships with the catering manager but I stuck it for a while.

By now I was finding my feet back in Haywards Heath. While I'd been working as a cook I'd become friendly with an older gay guy in the town, Roland. One day we saw a small piece in a local newspaper. It was only a little article half an inch by two inches and it was about a new social group, Gays, in mid Sussex. It was exactly what it said on the tin! It was a meeting place for gay people in my area. The advert said that the inaugural meeting was a few nights away, in an upstairs room at one of the local pubs, the Burrell Arms.

Roland and I went along. There were twenty people there which was amazing. You have to understand how bold this was back then. It was still the early 1980s. There was a gay community in Brighton, but for people to be openly gay in a small town like Haywards Heath was unheard of.

There were some really great people there; in particular, two guys – John and Jon – both very interesting and funny in their late forties. And the group expanded really rapidly. *Gay News* wrote a feature about this little community, which – again – was a measure of how unusual it was at the time. It became well known and was given an acronym: GYMS.

It turned into a vibrant social club. We'd go to the croquet lawns in Lewes, we'd meet with other gay groups in the south of England.

The group gave me a real sense of purpose and direction in my life at that time. I became quite political. It was a period when gay rights were coming to the fore. I joined the Gay Pride march in London each year and also worked for a charity, the Brighton Gay Switchboard, counselling people who were wrestling with many of the problems I'd faced. The GYMS community was good for me in so many ways. It even landed me a new job.

One day one of the Johns, Jon Gorman, asked me whether I'd be interested in a job at a local department store called George Hilton. I said yes, naturally. A couple of days later I went along for an interview with the new general manager of the store, a lady called Liz Palmer. She saw that I had experience in sales but gave me a temporary job as a warehouse porter down in Burgess Hill. She said that when she got a sales vacancy I would be the first option. I jumped at the opportunity and gleefully told the catering manager at the Home to shove her job where the sun didn't shine.

I thought the new job would get me back on the ladder so set out to impress. When I got to the warehouse I found that the dispatch department was a complete mess and reorganised the entire department, devising a new system. Liz was mightily impressed. Within a few months there was a sales vacancy in the furniture department. She was as good as her word and gave it to me.

I rose through the ranks of the department store rapidly. I was working in the furniture department and from there graduated into the carpet department, where I became the buyer, which was fantastic. I loved my job – it was a fun place to work, a real throwback to the world of *Are You Being Served*?

Jon told me a funny story about a woman who could have been Mrs Slocombe from the BBC television series. She was just that bit older than everyone else and worked in the make-up department where she wore just a bit too much eyeliner and lipstick. One day she'd been approached by an American lady who was asking about a very fashionable new lipstick from one of the big-name fashion houses.

'How much is it?' the woman asked.

'Twelve pound fifty, madam,' the shop assistant replied.

'My God, we can buy a lipstick twice that size for that money in the States,' the American lady said.

Quick as a flash, the assistant fixed her with a stare and said: 'In this country we make lipsticks for the size of women's mouths.'

Jon used to be a real practical joker and managed to fool me good and proper one day. I'd managed to sell a very nice glass and brass tea trolley to a titled lady who regularly visited the store. I was really pleased with myself about it. The trolley cost several hundred pounds. I accepted a cheque from the lady and then filled in the delivery details.

As I was making my way back to the office to register the sale Jon collared me. 'You haven't accepted a cheque from Lady X, have you?' he said.

'What do you mean?'

'You should never take a cheque off her – they always bounce,' he said, before sliding off.

I was panic stricken. For the next hour or so I was rehearsing what I was going to say to the general manager when – inevitably – I got hauled up for accepting a rubber cheque.

I was just about ready to do it when Jon drifted past me again. 'Didn't believe that about the cheque, did you?' he laughed. I could have throttled him.

By the time I was reaching my twentieth birthday I felt I had a job I could be proud of. I could feel my self-esteem returning again.

But there was a part of me that had felt very humiliated. I'd lost everything. Yet whenever I started to dwell on this I could hear Ida in my head. I could hear her saying, 'You need to have some grey hairs.' Looking back on that phase in my life now I can see that life – and maybe the spirit world – had been teaching me an important lesson or two. It might have been showing me that you have to experience the bad times to be able to enjoy the good ones. It wouldn't be the last time I'd learn this lesson, of course. But because it was the first time it made it a very powerful and potent piece of knowledge.

It is certainly an experience I have been able to draw upon ever since. There is a strong element of counselling in mediumship. Over the years I have frequently found myself in a position where I am providing emotional guidance for people. When people say to me now, 'I am never going to get over this,' or 'I won't be able to forget about that' I can tell them, 'Yes, you will, things do get better, what you are feeling now will pass.'

I know, because that's how I felt. And I am still here to tell the tale.

8 | A New Purpose

ONE afternoon in the early 1980s, when I was twenty-one or so, I caught a train from Haywards Heath down to Brighton. I was heading down to see a couple of old friends and to do a bit of shopping. The train was very quiet. Climbing on board, I could see there were only half a dozen people in my carriage.

As I walked through the train looking for a decent seat I noticed a young woman in her late twenties. Her body language was telling. She was sitting tight against the window, her head leaning against the glass, her face fixed in a joyless expression as she stared out at the passing countryside. She seemed extremely unhappy.

Out of nowhere I got a very powerful urge to sit opposite her. As I sat down I began picking up a very strong sense of another woman trying to connect with me psychically. I hadn't felt this way for some time, but the message was clear to me almost immediately. I needed to speak to this young woman.

This presented me with a tricky problem. I knew that it would seem extremely strange if I just suddenly blurted out what I was picking up. She would think I was some kind of nutcase. But, at the same time, I couldn't risk waiting too long in case she got off at the next stop, which was only a couple of minutes away.

The fates – or maybe the spirit world – soon solved my problem for me, however. As I was taking off my coat and settling back into my seat the train lurched to a sudden stop, throwing me slightly forward so that I almost fell into her lap.

'Oops, sorry,' I said.

'It's OK,' she said with a shy smile.

It was a perfect opportunity to strike up a conversation. 'Heading to Brighton?' I said, as I sat down again.

'Yeah,' she replied. 'If we ever get there.'

The train was still standing still and there had been no announcement from the guard, so we started making small talk.

The woman told me she was going to meet a friend who lived on a street near where Ida lived.

'Oh, I know where you mean,' I said. 'I used to attend a Spiritualist church near there.'

This seemed to pique her interest a little. 'Yes, I know that church. I went there once,' she said. 'How often do you go there?'

'Not as often as I used to,' I said. 'I had been training with one of the mediums there, but have stopped going for a bit while I sort out a few personal problems.'

'Really,' she said. 'Well, I'm sure you could get back

into it really easily. I'm sure you don't lose the knack,' she smiled.

'Probably not,' I said, sensing the conversation was heading in the right direction.

'So you could do a reading for me,' she said, looking out of the window as we sat, still motionless, on the tracks in the Sussex countryside.

'Well it's funny you should say that,' I said. 'I had actually received a message already.'

'Really,' she said, looking a little sceptical.

'I think it's from your mum,' I said.

She said nothing.

I went on to give her some details that established it was her mother. I told her that the lady had passed a year or so ago after a brief illness. She got quite emotional at this.

'That's right,' she said, reaching for a handkerchief.

I sensed she had been through a long and painful grieving process and her mum must have been very close to her.

'So what is she saying to me?' she said, using the handkerchief to dab away a tear.

I took a deep breath and passed on the message that I'd received a few minutes earlier. 'There is one thing that your mother wants you to know. This boyfriend that you have, you must leave him, because any man who hits a woman isn't worth being with.'

The expression on her face changed immediately. 'How does she know that?' she asked me.

'Because she is watching over you and wants the best for you,' I said.

It took a moment or two for her to digest all this. I felt her mother's energy levels waning fast so quickly shared one or two other personal messages with her daughter.

'She wants you to know that she is proud of you,' I told her as I felt the connection disappear altogether. This brought a smile to her face.

Soon after that the train lurched into life again. Before long we arrived in Brighton, and she began to get off. But before she left the carriage she just leaned over and kissed me.

'Thank you so much, that means so much to me, you have no idea how much that has helped me,' she said.

'Oh, I'm so glad,' I said. 'To be honest, I think you've helped me a little as well.'

I felt a huge sense of satisfaction. I felt like I had done the right thing. But I also felt something else. I realised that I was still able to tune into the spirit world as effectively as I had a year and a half earlier. In fact, if anything I had interpreted this message as clearly and accurately as any I'd received during my training with Ida.

'She's right, you don't lose the knack,' I said quietly to myself. And at that moment I made a decision.

It had been around a year and a half now since I

had been to a Spiritualist church. I had lost contact with Ida and everyone else I'd known there. My relationship with Chris, my mini-breakdown and half-hearted attempt at suicide had taken me away from all that. In my confused state, a part of me had blamed the spirit world for what had happened.

In the past I'd been given help when I needed it. But I hadn't seen the figures of my grandfather or the old man at the foot of the bed during that period. I hadn't heard the voice of the lady whispering, 'Not long.' I didn't sense very much at all in a psychic sense. So I'd concluded that the spirit world had somehow abandoned me.

As I got myself back together again I realised that it was the other way around: it was me that had abandoned the spirit world. And as I regained my equilibrium I realised that had been a mistake. It was an important part of my life, one that I needed to connect with if I was going to be a happy and rounded person.

So that Sunday I headed down to Brighton again. I went to the church that Ida worked at most often and, sure enough, she was there.

I approached her after the service and gave her a sheepish smile. 'Hello, remember me?' I said, slightly apologetically.

'Oh, hello. I knew you'd come back eventually,' she smiled.

Afterwards we had a cup of tea and caught up on

what had been happening in each other's lives. She'd not been in the best of health and had discontinued her circle for a period. When I told her about all the trouble I'd had she just nodded wisely. I remembered her prediction the last time we'd seen each other. She would have been perfectly entitled to say, 'I told you so,' but she didn't.

We sat and chatted for what must have been half an hour. It was cathartic.

At one point I told her about the difficulties my coming out had caused in my family, with my father in particular.

'I know what you are going through,' she said. 'I've had problems with my family because of who I am.'

I knew very little about Ida's family background. She explained to me that she had been forced to sacrifice her relationship with her own children because of her mediumship. She had two daughters, neither of whom had any interest in her work, and one of whom had actively turned against her by becoming a Jehovah's Witness. Of her nearest and dearest, only Ida's sister had been supportive of her work.

'That must have been so difficult for you,' I said.

'It was. But they had to follow their path and I have to follow mine. I have to be true to what I do and who I am.'

It was then that she said something profound, something that I've never forgotten and have, in fact, used as a balancing point in my life ever since. 'Colin, people will come into your life and they will go out of your life again. That's true on this side of life and beyond death. You will form very intense relationships and friendships, but you have to remember that people are sent into each other's lives to serve a purpose,' she said. 'And I think your purpose is to be a medium.'

She said that there was every chance Chris and I would rekindle our relationship one day. 'You've gone your separate ways now, but it doesn't mean that you won't come together again. The important thing is that you must never try to hold on to people in life after they have served their purpose. You have to let them go.'

That conversation with Ida was prescient in all sorts of ways. As I turned twenty-one and 'came of age', I felt like life was beginning to take shape for me. I had a decent job, a group of good friends, and my development as a medium was really getting somewhere. I celebrated my birthday with my friends from GYMS, who organised a party at my friend Roland's flat. They had clubbed together for a couple of presents and gave me a gold cigarette lighter and a T-shirt that read 'Legal at Last'. I still have it at the bottom of a drawer somewhere.

My early twenties were a happy time in the main, focussed on my community and political activism. I was very happy. Life has a habit of kicking you when you least expect it, however. Around the time I was twenty-three I became partially deaf.

It started off innocuously enough. I had been having a lot of pain in my jaw and went to see the dentist. He took a look at me and announced that I had impacted wisdom teeth.

'They will have to come out, I'm afraid, Mr Fry,' he said.

'OK, well if you want to do it now that's fine,' I replied rather naively.

'No, you'll need to go into hospital to have it done,' he said. 'It's quite a major operation.'

I went into work and told my boss and colleagues that I'd need a few days off to have my wisdom teeth removed. Everyone laughed, cracking jokes about how I'd look like a hamster when I came back. I took it all light-heartedly. What could go wrong? It was only a routine operation, after all.

I was booked into the old Cuckfield Hospital. I turned up and was told I'd be kept in overnight and released the following day. I wasn't particularly nervous but my mum came with me. A couple of hours after I'd been checked in the consultant who was going to be conducting the operation came to see me. I might have imagined it, but I was convinced that he stank of whisky.

The next morning I was prepared for the operation and wheeled into surgery. When I came round I didn't feel right at all. It wasn't just the pain, which I'd known to expect. There was something else that didn't feel right.

I was discharged the following day but was still feeling a constant pain. There was this massive pressure behind my ears and I couldn't hear properly.

I was having dinner a couple of nights later when I felt this awful searing pain in my mouth. To my mother and father's horror, I pulled out a two-inch-long shard of bone from my mouth.

'What on earth is that?' I said to my mother, knowing that, as a nurse, she might have a good idea.

'Oh, my Lord. They've splintered your jaw,' she said.

So she rang the hospital and explained that there had been a fracturing of the bone during the operation and that this splinter had come through the gum. They didn't seem terribly concerned and told my mother that I should go and see the doctor if it hadn't got any better in a couple of days' time. The pain didn't ease, however. But I couldn't face going back to the doctor's. Instead I went back to work still feeling this pain behind my ears.

It was on the second day that a colleague of mine turned to me in the morning and said: 'Colin, you don't look right. Why don't you have an early coffee break and see if you feel better.'

I had a coffee and was walking back to the furniture department where I worked, when I passed out. It was decided I should be taken to hospital and a senior member of staff took me to Cuckfield Hospital. Apparently I'd collapsed on the floor with blood coming out of my ears.

I was given some heavy medication and told to rest. But whenever I came around I realised I couldn't hear anything. Literally nothing. I had gone totally deaf in both ears and stayed that way for the next four days.

A doctor examined me but said he could see nothing and sent me home.

For the next four days all I could hear was this buzzing. It was awful. The thing about losing your hearing is that your sense of perception goes as well. You can't even hear a cup being placed on a table. Over the next couple of days I broke a couple of cups because I was slamming them down rather than placing them carefully. My mum and dad had to write things down for me so that I could understand.

My mother and other friends with medical knowledge were convinced that my ears had been traumatised by the experience of the operation and the fracturing of the jaw but that my hearing would come back. They were partly right. After about four or five days, it slowly started to come back. But the buzzing remained – and never went away. Ever since then my hearing comes and goes: one moment I can hear everything just fine, the next I can't hear a thing.

Eventually a private specialist in Brighton diagnosed it as a case of tinnitus with hearing loss. I have had to deal with it ever since.

I was convinced that the damage had been done by the whisky-breathed consultant and, for a while, thought about seeking compensation. At one point, they sent me to Kings College Hospital for a week to try to establish what was wrong. Early on during my stay there, one of the doctors said he thought that something had gone seriously wrong during the operation and that perhaps I should consider taking action against the surgeon. He soon backtracked on that advice, however.

On the last day of my stay I went to see a consultant. As I waited to go into the consultant's office I heard raised voices. It was the doctor who had been looking after me. He was saying: 'With all due respect, sir, that's not right.' His meaning soon became clear.

When I came into the room, the consultant said, 'Mr Fry, we can't find anything wrong so we suggest you go away and see a psychiatrist.'

I looked at the doctor and said, 'Do you agree with this?'

He simply said, 'I can't comment.'

Coincidently, the surgeon who did the operation was given early retirement. But I'm convinced that he was drunk when he operated on me. He should have split the wisdom teeth and taken them out in sections but he took them out in one piece instead.

The legacy of the botched operation stayed with me from then on. I was prescribed hearing aids and, at first, had to wear the old-fashioned ones that hook over your ears, which I hated, mainly because it encouraged people to come up to me and shout in my ear. To this day I have to wear hearing aids on stage because I don't want to be halfway through a performance and suddenly not be able to hear anything. Thankfully, they are a little more sophisticated and discreet these days.

Despite my illness, I was doing well at work. The fact that I now had a steady, reasonably well paid job meant that I could think about leaving home again. I was in my early twenties and eager to get on with life. I didn't want to be still living with my parents, even though life was comfortable there.

At first I put myself down for a council house, but it was soon clear I wouldn't be offered a flat. I was a single man – it was unbelievable how far down the pecking order in their waiting lists I was. But then I learned about a new, shared-ownership scheme under which you bought your house in partnership with the council. There were quite a few properties available under this scheme in Haywards Heath. All I needed to do was raise a deposit. I took on extra work, including three nights a week in a pub called The Golden Eagle. The landlords, Ray and Barbara, were exceptionally nice people, with whom I got on famously.

Soon I'd saved up most of the deposit. But I needed another £1,500 for the other costs. Barbara and Ray were incredibly generous and gave me £1,000. My friends John and Jon from GYMS gave me the other £500 as a loan for my solicitor's fees. Soon I was on the property ladder. It wasn't a palace; far from it, it was a small, modern, terraced house. It was more like a rabbit hutch. But it was my rabbit hutch. I moved in with a fridge, a beanbag and a sleeping bag.

I then threw my first ever housewarming party. Lots of friends from Haywards Heath, Brighton and beyond came up. Michael, the two Johns and my workmates came along as well. And so, too, did Chris.

Chris and I had remained on friendly terms. Deep down, I had never really got over him. I had not had a serious boyfriend since him and, even though my life was becoming successful, I didn't want anyone other than him. When I'd had a glass of wine too many, I would often talk about him. My friends must have got totally fed up with it.

Chris and I talked a lot at the party, catching up on what had been going on in each other's lives. I refused to wear my hearing aids for the occasion, so he had to shout quite loudly over the blaring music at one point. But we both realised that we still had feelings for each other. Our relationship was rekindled.

Initially he would come up to see me every other weekend. My father wasn't very pleased that I was back with this guy who, as far as he was concerned, had caused so many problems. But, again, I was led by my heart and not my head. I had soon asked Chris to move in with me. He waited until he got a job locally, working for the Post Office, before making the move up from Brighton.

We had a little two-bedroomed terraced house and a dog called Lady, who was a cross between a Border Collie and a Labrador. It was a new life, one that – for a while, at least – made me happy.

One day I spotted an advert for a job with the Stone family, for whose carpet firm I'd worked years earlier. They now had three carpet shops in Burgess Hill, Eastbourne and Portslade, near Brighton. It was a decent job with a good salary, so I sent in an application, expecting a written reply in a few days. Almost immediately I got a phone call from the wife of the MD, Barbara Stone, asking me to come over and see them.

Eric Stone Senior had passed away, leaving his sons to run the company. I met his son, Eric Junior, as he was known, and Barbara and I chatted, catching up on old times. They offered me a job on the spot and I had soon progressed to managing the Portslade branch. Eric Junior had put me in charge when his brother Greg had been ill. He'd been so impressed he'd made me manager.

The family knew I was a medium and were fascinated by it. But I made a strict rule with myself that I never mixed work and my 'extra-curricular' activities. During my time with the Stone family I bent that rule just twice.

The first occasion came one day when we got a phone call from a lady who wanted some bathroom carpet. She lived on the far side of Brighton, towards Peacehaven. I checked to see who was available in the warehouse or shop, but to my disappointment found there was no one who could go and measure the carpet. So I just thought to myself: 'I am going to have to go.' I wasn't too pleased by this. I had a million and one things to do back in the warehouse. 'All this for the sake of a piece of carpet that might only be three foot by six foot,' I muttered to myself.

I got to the address to be greeted by an elderly lady. She seemed very subdued, almost sad. As I made it a policy always to be helpful and charming, I went into sales mode and explained to her that she needed a rubber-backed carpet for the bathroom and produced some samples that I'd brought along. She looked through them, rather half-heartedly, eventually choosing one.

'I don't know why I am bothering really – my husband has just passed away so it's just me on my own,' she sighed as I did the paperwork to confirm the order.

'I know, George passed over earlier this year,' I said, without even thinking.

'How do you know my husband's name?' she said, startled.

'Oh, sugar,' I said to myself. 'Why did I do that?'

I had no intention of giving her a message. It had

just happened. The minute I'd walked through the door I'd been aware that there had been some kind of death connected to this house. I felt strongly that she was a widow. And when she'd made her comment the name was there in my head.

Her mood quickly changed. I felt I had to tell her that I was a medium. Her reaction was to ask me to go on and tell her what else I could sense. So I proceeded to tell her that George sent his love and best wishes and that he thought she should do more to get out and get on with her life.

As I'd suspected, the order I got was for a small piece of carpet. It would hardly justify the petrol and the time I'd spent in driving there. But I was even more concerned about what I'd done. As I got into the van and drove back I thought, 'I shouldn't have done that.' I had made a promise to myself not to allow one side of my life to interfere with the other. I worried about it all the way back and for days afterwards.

A few days later Greg, the director at the time, called me into the office. He told me to sit down then handed me a letter. 'I think you'd better read this,' he said.

It was from the lady's daughter. 'One of your staff came to measure up for a carpet for my mother. I can't tell you how happy he has made my mother. He has a wonderful gift and if he does private sittings my mother and I would like to see him,' she wrote.

I started to apologise to Greg before I'd even

finished the letter. I was terrified he thought I was using his family's company to drum up business for my other line of work.

'I never intended for that side of my life to interfere with my work. It just happened,' I said.

He shrugged his shoulders. 'Honestly, Colin, I'm not worried about it. We know you wouldn't deliberately do it. You've done a wonderful thing for the woman,' he said.

Not many employers would have been so understanding. After that I swore to myself that I wouldn't let it happen again. But within less than a year, it had.

One May morning a couple came into the showroom looking for some carpet for their flat in Hove. They were both elderly, she was in a wheelchair. I'd served them and had spent a long time finding the right shade and texture of carpet. I'd given them a quote and agreed to go along to their flat the following day.

I was in their home the next day when I was struck by an overwhelming sense that it was a significant place spiritually. As I walked around with my tape measure, all I could hear was this nagging voice saying, 'Tell him that you know he uses this room for seances.' At first I resisted. I didn't want a repeat of what had happened in Peacehaven. But it wouldn't go away so eventually I rather nervously approached the man. 'You use this room for seances, don't you,' I said as politely as possible.

I'd expected him to be shocked, surprised or maybe even offended. But instead he just looked at me calmly and said, 'Yes, and how do you know that?'

'Because a spirit voice just told me,' I said.

It was the beginning of one of the longest and most significant relationships in my mediumistic life. The man immediately told his wife, who smiled and said that 'they knew I was coming'.

Over a cup of tea they introduced themselves as John and Geraldine Austin. They told me that they had been running regular development circles for many years. The family's interest in Spiritualism went back even further: John's mother had run a circle many years earlier. I explained that I'd initially developed my abilities at Ida's circle. They had heard of her but explained that they took more of an interest in physical and trance mediumship than the mental mediumship that she'd taught me. They admitted that they were finding it difficult to fill their group at that time and invited me to join them at their next Tuesday evening circle.

'I don't know whether I will be any good at it,' I told them. Again they smiled as if to say they knew something that I didn't.

They explained that a trance medium from the North of England had visited their circle some time earlier and brought through a spirit that predicted my arrival fairly accurately. It had said that a young medium would visit the house in May and make himself known. The members of the circle had been instructed to develop me further because they had 'big plans for me'.

The following week I went to John and Geraldine's flat for what would be the first of many, many evenings together. They were looking for others to join the circle so I suggested Pat, my former neighbour with whom I'd remained on good terms and who still took a really keen interest in the subject. Together with a local guy called Lennie and one or two others, we formed a circle that remained intact for many years.

Sitting in a development circle can be a long, arduous and boring process. Often you sit for hours in the darkness or with a red light on, waiting for something to happen. And often it doesn't. Fortunately for us, however, things did begin to happen – almost immediately.

As they had predicted, I demonstrated an ability for trance mediumship. On the second evening we sat together I had experienced this strange sleepiness, as if I was nodding off. When I'd pulled myself together, I was informed that two hours had passed, during which time I'd passed on a series of messages, many of them in the voice of the spirit who was communicating.

'But I don't remember anything,' I'd said to John.

'No, you wouldn't,' he explained. 'During that time your mind is basically inhabited by spirit – or spirits. You have no memory of it afterwards.'

I was fascinated to hear what had happened and was amazed when John told me that I'd passed on a message from John and Geraldine's son. I didn't even know they had a son, but John explained that he had been killed in a train accident years earlier. He had been heading up to a West End play in London and was running late. John had told him to sit in the front of the train so as to make a quick getaway at the other end. The front of the train took the brunt of the impact in the crash, while those at the back emerged from the wreckage with hardly a scratch.

John and Geraldine had suffered a massive crisis of faith after this. They had both been very active in the Spiritualist church but turned their back on it. Like many people who suffer a shocking loss, they couldn't understand how their God had allowed it to happen.

Slowly but surely, however, they had reconnected with Spiritualism, partly in the hope that they would one day make a connection with their son. The fact that I had enabled them to do this was a hugely emotional moment for them. It cemented the bond that was already forming between us. John, Geraldine and I became very close. Geraldine passed over a couple of years after I joined their circle, but even with her gone, I learned a huge amount from those regular Tuesday evenings.

Ida's group had been very much for 'fledglings', apprentices. Here I was treated as an adult and allowed free rein to explore my abilities. As I did so I learned so much about the gift that I'd been carrying with me since I was a child – and about the spirits who had been guiding me since those early days in Wivelsfield.

Ever since I'd joined Ida's circle I'd secretly hoped that one night I might encounter the old, grey-haired man who had sat at the foot of my bed since I was a four-year-old. Ida had told me that he was almost certainly my spirit guide, the person on the other side dedicated to leading me to enlightenment. But I'd never learned much more than that.

This changed as I began to develop as a trance medium with Geraldine and John. When I went into a trance, I apparently spoke in a number of voices. According to John, some of these were spirit guides. The popular notion of spirit guides is of these colourful characters – Amazonian Indians, Native Americans, Egyptians and Roman soldiers, for example. But more often than not they are more mundane people. And so it was with me. Mine consisted of a doctor and school-teacher. I did have one more exotic one, a Chinese alchemist. However, the one that came through most consistently was a Victorian gentleman whose name was Magnus.

It had taken me almost twenty years to discover this, so I wasn't that concerned when Magnus proved reluctant to tell me too much about himself at one time. At first he revealed that he was a publisher who had lived in London in the nineteenth century, with offices in Bloomsbury, the centre of the book trade in the Victorian era. During another visit he revealed that he had been born in Edinburgh, but had left Scotland when he was a young baby and his parents separated.

What was great and liberating about my development at John and Geraldine's circle was that it was teaching me how to use my abilities in a wide number of ways. I now found myself able to talk to Magnus – and other spirits – more easily. Around this time I regularly talked to him. His presence was always there. Magnus taught me a great deal about the spirit world and its workings. Apparently he was allocated to me as a guide when I was born, being given the role by what he calls The Enlightened Ones. His role early on was to be a 'watcher', literally watching over me. When I began to experiment with mental mediumship with Ida he was around a little more, ensuring that I didn't make any terrible mistakes. Now that I had begun to practise as a trance medium, however, he was going to be much more present.

As I got to know Magnus I discovered he could be a difficult character. There were times when he was short-tempered and quite snappy with me. But I also learned that he had a deeply compassionate side that had been moulded by an experience he had with a maid in his house in Victorian London. He had sacked her in a fit of temper, condemning her to a life of poverty which she hadn't survived for long. He'd met her when he'd passed over to the other side and had been overwhelmed by her forgiveness. Since then Magnus had been a member of a collective of souls called 'The Diamond'. His existence was now dedicated to making amends for his mistakes during his life and offering guidance that ensured others, like me, didn't make similar errors during their time in this earthly realm.

'You've had your work cut out with me,' I said to him once.

9 | Centre of Attention

TURNING up for the weekly circle one Tuesday evening, I noticed a new member of the group, a quite distinguished-looking man in a dark jacket. 'Colin, this is Robin,' John said to me. 'He's joining us for the evening. He's very interested in your development.'

'OK,' I said, thinking little of it. I was more concerned with getting ready for the evening's seance. The evening proceeded along the usual lines. The spirit world operates at a higher level of vibration than the earthly realm. So we would always begin with a prayer and some singing, to raise the vibration levels. I would then go into a trance and pass on whatever communications came through to me. I did so again tonight.

That evening, apparently, I connected with a range of people, including someone that this man Robin had known well. Afterwards, as we sipped the customary cup of tea in the kitchen, he came over to me and John. 'Hello, Colin, we weren't really introduced properly beforehand, my name is Robin Foy,' he said.

I was taken aback. I'd heard of him, he was quite prominent in psychic circles. I'd read about him in the psychic press and I knew that he lived in a large house in the Norfolk village of Scole, where he had converted a large cellar into a seance room. There were rumours of all sorts of physical phenomena being witnessed there, from tiny globes of light, to floating robes to spirit hands that had physically touched people. It sounded fascinating.

'I don't suppose you've heard of the Noah's Ark Society?' Robin asked me.

As it happened, I had, mainly thanks to John, who was a member. The Society had formed quite recently and was named after a man called Noah Zerdin, who was a spirit mentor to one of Britain's best known mediums, Leslie Flint. It was purported that through a trance medium Noah had come through and spoken to Robin Foy, instructing him to form a society for the safe practice of physical mediumship. When I explained this to Robin, he just smiled.

'Ah, good,' he said. 'That saves me some time. The reason I came to see you tonight is that I'd like to invite you and John to attend our first seminar, up in Leicester in a few weeks' time.'

I wasn't sure I had the time, or the inclination, but he seemed very keen for me to go.

'I think a lot of people would be very interested to see what you are capable of doing,' he said.

'I'll give it some thought,' I said.

Over the coming days John and Pat both rang me to tell me what a big opportunity – and an honour – this could be for me. John, in particular, explained what a significant event this seminar was going to be. Physical mediumship, in which spirits manifest themselves literally in a physical way, had been hugely popular during the latter part of the nineteenth and early part of the twentieth century. Since then, however, it had faded out, partly because of the bad publicity it had received because of the activities of a few fraudsters. The Spiritualist community had focused instead on mental mediumship, which had become the norm.

There were only a very few physical mediums left practising, the most famous of whom were Leslie Flint and Gordon Higginson, both elderly men. Many believed that once they passed over that would be it, the art would be lost. Which was why the Noah's Ark Society were so keen to revive and continue the art.

What they were attempting in Leicester was particularly ambitious, John told me. They had invited prominent psychics and mediums from all over the UK and beyond for a large, public display of physical mediumship.

'No one has tried anything like this in this country for something like sixty years,' John said to me. 'You'd be missing out on something amazing if you didn't come, Colin.'

I was soon persuaded.

*

A few weeks later, John, Pat and I travelled up to Leicester and booked into the hotel where the seminar was to be held. I was amazed at the number of people who were gathered in the lounge, lobby and bars. There must have been three hundred people there. I was also introduced to the leading lights of the Noah's Ark Society. There were some eminent names, including Alan Crossley who was well known in mediumistic circles for his experiences communicating with the late medium Helen Duncan. There was Robin, whom I'd met, and another man, George Cranley.

I took an instant dislike to George. He was a studious but slightly snooty figure, I thought. 'I'm hearing some very good reports about your ability, young man,' he said when we were introduced. He then looked over his glasses and said, 'But if you are a fraud I will have no problems in exposing you.'

'I don't like that man,' I said to John.

Ironically, George went on to be one of my greatest supporters and closest friends, being a real mentor for twenty years.

I also met a young guy called Tony Stockwell, who was nineteen at the time, a young medium from Essex. He too would play a part in my future.

At that point, however, I was more concerned with the present. During the evening before the seance I noticed that John and Pat seemed very edgy and nervous. I assumed it was to do with the concerns that people in general had about what was going to occur. At one point, we were talking with Alan Crossley about the room in which the seance was to be conducted. Conditions for a seance have to be very specific. The room has to be blacked out so that everything can be conducted in complete darkness.

'The conditions aren't right,' Alan Crossley told us. 'It's just a normal conference room with blackout blinds and curtains. I'm worried it's not good enough for what we want to do.'

I couldn't share their anxiety, however. I was revelling in the fact I was in the company of so many interesting people. The truth was I was being naive. It was only the following day that I discovered what was really about to unfold.

I had gone along assuming that I might be one of many mediums who would be involved in this demonstration. But as the time approached for the seance to begin, I realised that wasn't quite the case. I was the one and only medium.

A short time before the seance was about to begin, Robin Foy approached me and explained that he wanted me to do pretty much the same thing that I'd done when he'd come to see me in Hove. 'Just do what comes naturally to you. Let the spirit flow through you,' he said.

He explained that they were going to be using a few of the traditional techniques of physical mediumship from the 1920s and 1930s. They had made what is known as a seance trumpet, a normal-looking trumpet which is luminous at both ends. In the right circumstances, I was told, spirit will levitate it and speak through it. There were also some pens and pieces of paper put on the table in case the spirits present wanted to communicate that way.

Finally, my chair had extremely high tension cables attached to it, so that I would be tied down. I knew a bit about the reasoning behind this. Many years ago there was a very famous physical medium called Eusapia Palladino. She used to say, 'If you don't restrain me, I will cheat, not consciously.' I understand what she meant. I've given a lot of thought to this over the years. If you imagine in the production of physical mediumship everything has to be passed through the medium. And if the thought is being passed through the mind of the medium that a chair is to move, a table is to move or a trumpet is to lift, the human body will respond to that. If that instruction 'lift the trumpet in the air' appears to you, you are going to do that before the spirit can bypass you and do what it is supposed to do. So mediums had to be strapped in to avoid the perception of fraud.

What they were hoping to happen was literally phenomenal. There hadn't been an experiment like this for sixty years. The last big public demonstration would have been by Leslie Flint in the 1930s. But even then he was a direct voice medium. He didn't deal in physical manifestations.

As the clock ticked down to the time when the seance was due to start and people were filing into the room, John and Pat helped me with the final preparations. I could tell they were nervous on my behalf. I think they sensed that I was too young and inexperienced for what was about to happen. John, in particular, had a lot of experience of physical mediumship and knew the conditions just weren't favourable at all. 'Are you sure you want to go through with this, Colin?' he whispered in my ear. 'You can walk away now if you want to.'

But I had no qualms. 'It's fine,' I said.

I really couldn't understand their concern. If all I had to do was replicate what I did in Hove each week, then what did I have to fear? I had always risen to a challenge, and still do. When I'm confronted with a challenge my attitude as a medium is to allow whatever is going to happen to happen. I wasn't intimidated or scared.

As we prepared to begin, I could see why Alan Crossley and others had been concerned about the conditions. We couldn't black the entire place out so we were only in half darkness rather than complete darkness. So I sat there and let the normal process that had been happening in circle begin: I let the spirit take control of me and I went into a trance state. Two hours later, I was cut free and taken from the room. I was taken into a room and left to rest for twenty minutes or so.

When I rejoined everyone, it was obvious immediately that it had gone well. John and Pat had come to collect me from the room and were the first to congratulate me. Pat was a little bit emotional about it. She couldn't believe the little boy who'd visited her house to look at some puppies all those years ago had been at the centre of something so extraordinary.

'So what happened?' I asked.

John began describing to me how it had begun with voices speaking through me and the trumpet levitating. But before he could finish, other people were coming into the room, all eager to shake my hand and give me a pat on the back.

'Well done, young man,' George Cranley said. 'I think it's fair to say that you surpassed all expectations.'

For the next few minutes a stream of people flowed into the room, each telling me something new about what had happened. It continued through that evening and the following morning.

The most moving conversation I had was with a middle-aged lady, the day after the seance. She had had a communication from her son, Richard. He had died in a car accident a couple of years earlier. She'd attended a number of seances and private sittings with mediums but had never received a message. She was very emotional about finally making contact with him.

At one point, she told me, she had actually felt him taking her by the hand. Even more amazingly, the trumpet had levitated over her head and she had been told to hold out her hands. As she did so, a piece of very soft, almost tissue-like paper fell into her hand.

When it was opened up after the seance it had the words 'Mummy, I love you, Richard' written out in handwriting but in tiny black dots.

That morning she'd been to see George Cranley and some other members of the committee to show them something she'd brought along in her handbag. It was the last birthday card her son had given her while he was alive. When they compared the writing in the card with the dotted writing on the tissue paper they found it was exactly the same. It was a perfect match.

Everyone left Leicester in high spirits. The committee members thanked me for coming and said they would be in touch about organising some more seances.

'Maybe,' I thought to myself. 'It's been a pleasant weekend. I wouldn't mind doing it again.'

In my naivety, I really hadn't realised the importance of what had happened. I headed back down to Sussex thinking it had been just another seance. But it hadn't been. I soon discovered that all hell was about to break loose.

The seance became big, big news in the psychic community. Over the next few weeks it was in all the leading publications: *Psychic News* ran a big piece, as did *Two Worlds* magazine and other psychic and Spiritualist magazines around the world.

Hundreds of letters arrived from around the world, all of them addressed to John's flat in Hove and all directed to a man called 'Lincoln'. The Noah's Ark Society had, in their wisdom, decided that I had to remain anonymous. To be fair to them, they were acting in my best interests. So they'd come up with the name, which was an anagram of Colin, well almost.

I found it a bit disconcerting. On the one hand, I had to lead a double life. To those who knew me locally as a medium, I was Colin Fry. But to the wider world, I was Lincoln, this 'wonder kid' medium. It was a bit odd. But I was also uncomfortable with it because I couldn't correct some of the stuff that was being written about me. Everyone was writing about how 'Lincoln's abilities have developed so quickly', for instance. Well, I had been working at it for quite a while, and John and Geraldine had been running their circle for more than twenty years.

But, for the moment, I agreed to continue in anonymity. It couldn't last forever, though.

Around this time, I also got invited to run a development class in a bookshop in Brighton called The Mystic Rainbow. Strangely, it was opposite the carpet shop that I used to run there. I jumped at the chance and started to run a development class on Friday night. About thirty people came each week. It became very popular.

One of the regulars there was a lady called Sylvia McRobb, who was quite prominent in the local

Spiritualist Church movement. She and I became very friendly, so much so that before she passed over she asked me to conduct her funeral service, which was a huge honour for me.

One evening at The Mystic Rainbow, I decided to do a talk on physical mediumship. To the vast majority of people with an interest in Spiritualism, this was still very much a mystery. No one had seen it practised. All they could do was read about it in *Psychic News* and old books. I drew on my own experience and gave this talk, which went down very well.

As it was drawing to a close, and I invited questions from the floor, Sylvia stood up and asked a question.

'You seem very knowledgeable about this, Colin,' she said, congratulating me on the talk. 'Have you heard of this amazing young medium called Lincoln? I'm a member of the Noah's Ark Society and I'm hoping to see him first hand at some point. Apparently his mediumship is quite extraordinary.'

As she spoke, I couldn't stop myself from laughing.

'Why are you laughing? What's so funny?' Sylvia said, looking a little bit peeved.

'Sylvia, I'm laughing because I am Lincoln.'

You could have heard a pin drop. Her face was a picture.

The impact the Leicester seance had on my life was immense. I got invitations to demonstrate at Spiritualist churches and in public demonstrations up and down the country. There was no doubt, however, that by far the most significant invitation I got was from Britain's greatest living medium, Leslie Flint.

It came about in quite a complicated way, via a friend I'd made in my home circle, the actress Carol Hawkins. I'd met her after a rather memorable message had come through from her former colleague on the *Carry On* films, the late, great Kenneth Williams. He'd been trying to get in contact with her and had come through at our regular Tuesday evening session. Before we'd been able to make an attempt to contact her, she'd rung us, asking whether she could sit in a circle with me. The spirit world had clearly been determined that we get together.

Her first visit had been a memorable one. Kenneth Williams had come through again and, through me in trance, had spoken directly to Carol. He'd explained that he'd been suffering from terrible depression before passing in 1988 and had lived up to the promise he'd made when he was alive not to 'hang around' when he felt his time had come. He'd expressed a lot of regret about the way he'd behaved towards the end of his life, particularly towards his sister, who had been left to clear up the mess after his passing. Carol had been delighted to receive this message and we'd subsequently become close. She and her husband, Martyn, had opened a couple of spiritual shops in Surrey and were already talking to me about attending to run some seances there.

It was some time after the Leicester seance that Carol rang me out of the blue one morning. 'Colin, Leslie Flint would like you to conduct a seance at his home,' she said.

'Really,' I said. I was flabbergasted. Leslie Flint was one of my heroes. I'd been fortunate to see him on a couple of occasions when I was developing with Ida and he'd brought through a message from my grandfather, Lawrie. I was slightly in awe of him. I told Carol I'd be honoured to do it. A few moments later she rang back with a date.

A few days later, along with Carol, Martyn, Pat and John, I went along to Leslie's home in Hove, where he'd retired to spend his final days. My nerves were jangling. For some reason, it felt more stressful than the Noah's Ark Society seminar in Leicester. I suppose it was because I was being asked to conduct a seance for the master of the art.

Arriving at Leslie's home, the other guests didn't help to ease my nerves. I remembered from attending Leslie's seances previously that the atmosphere was very formal, almost austere. Nobody spoke to each other. It was the same tonight. The others assembled in his drawing room were polite enough but very distant, as if they were unsure who I was and what I was doing there.

Eventually we went into Leslie's seance room where he appeared. He looked very pale and weak, as if he was clinging on to life. He was literally half the man I'd seen several years ago. I tried to stick that to the back of my mind and allowed myself to go into a trance. When I came around an hour or so later, the mood in the house had been transformed totally. The people who had been so reticent and distant from me were suddenly my best friends in the world. Even more dramatically, Leslie's demeanour had changed completely. It was as if he'd been taken back in time ten years. His face was full of colour and he seemed energised.

I soon discovered why.

'Come with me, young man,' he said, leading me towards a private room where we talked for a few minutes.

Leslie told me that he'd invited me over after hearing a tape-recording made at one of my regular trance seances at The Mystic Rainbow. While I was in trance, Magnus, my regular spirit guide, had made way for another spirit – that of Leslie's former partner, Bram, who had died suddenly months earlier. Bram had had a conversation with someone in the audience during which he had passed on a very specific message to Leslie. This person had been taping my seance and got the recording back to Leslie.

'Having heard the tape, I was convinced that it was Bram. Through you he made a comment about how I should use the silver bells at Christmas. Earlier that day I had said to someone that, with Christmas coming, I couldn't be bothered to hang the antique silver bells that I always placed on the tree when Bram was alive. He also called me Daddy, which was a pet nickname he had for me,' he said. He was in effusive mood and was really complimentary. 'I have heard good things about you, but one never knows until one sees a medium working at first hand. Now I know that you are every bit as good as they say you are,' he smiled.

It was a hugely important moment for me and my career. I did two other seances for Leslie, before he passed over in 1994. He also, without any prompting from me and to my complete surprise, wrote a long and glowing letter to *Psychic News*. In it he said that he had received many claims of contact with Bram since his passing, but that the only ones that he knew to be authentic were mine. 'Mr Fry gave me irrevocable evidence of Bram's survival,' he said. It was, in many ways, a more significant moment than the Leicester seance because he mentioned me by name. I was no longer obliged to hide behind the mask of Lincoln.

Leslie Flint has remained a role model for me ever since. I still have at home a copy of his famous book *Voices in the Dark*, in which he talks to that other great supporter of mine, George Cranley. Leslie told George that the purpose of a medium is: '. . . to help humanity, to give comfort from the point of view that death is not the end, that the person they've known and loved still exists and at times is able to come near them, and that one day they will meet again on the Other Side of life.'

Leslie also spoke about the 'great responsibility' all mediums carry with them. I still try to live up to his words to this day.

10 | Grey Hairs

ONE weekend in October 1992, I was invited back up to Robin Foy's home in Scole, Norfolk to take part in another seance with the Noah's Ark Society. I'd participated in several of these by now. They took place in front of an invited audience of thirty or forty people in Robin's specially converted seance room in the basement of his house. They had gone well and only added to the interest in the mysterious 'Lincoln', about whom everyone in the psychic community still seemed to be talking.

On this particular weekend I drove up with John for company. We'd made the trip a few times now and there was a familiar look to the flat, East Anglian countryside. As we reached the border of Norfolk, however, I sensed something unfamiliar, an energy I'd never felt before. It was very strong, and was making me feel uneasy. It was hard to describe, I can only categorise it as a 'psychic nausea'.

'I have a really bad feeling about this today, John,' I said, turning to him at one point.

'Really,' he said. 'Well, if you don't feel right you

shouldn't do it. We can cancel, if we stop and give Robin a call now there is still time. There are still a few hours to go.'

Everything in my bones was telling me that he was right, we should cancel. But I ignored it. 'No, we'd better press on, he's got forty people coming, some are apparently travelling from a long way away to be there tonight. I don't want to disappoint them.'

It was the most fateful decision of my life, one that would haunt me for the rest of my career.

The strange feeling remained with me all the way up to the gates of Robin's home in Scole. Even after I'd been greeted by Robin and his invited guests and I was being prepared for the seance, I had this nagging feeling that something wasn't right. But the pressure for me to 'perform' was now too great to resist. There were people there from all over the country. One person had made a ten-hour trip from the Isle of Man. A couple of people were booked into nearby hotels for the night. I couldn't let them down.

The arrangements tonight were the same as usual. I was to be tied and strapped into the chair, using 300 lb-pressure nylon cable ties, bound around my ankles and wrists. There was a collection of items laid out on the table in the hope they would attract the attention of any spirit that came through. In the past Robin had reported incidences of spirits throwing things and even playing musical instruments so the items included a bell, a keyboard, a bowl of molasses, an illuminated toy in the shape of an octopus and a couple of spirit trumpets.

Robin had designed the room with the utmost attention to detail. He knew that to get the best results it needed to be absolutely pitch-black during the seance. He also knew that for the lights to come on unexpectedly during the performance was extremely dangerous to the medium, especially if he or she was inhabited by spirit. So he had built a cabinet inside which the controls for the lights were kept. When the lights went out, the box was locked and would remain that way until the end of the seance.

The seance began, as they usually did, with the singing of hymns and other music to create the right vibrations. As was usual, I felt myself falling into a trance and can recall nothing else of what happened, but some of those who had attended regularly later reported that from the beginning it didn't feel right. Apparently the guides who came through didn't sound right and the phenomena were aggressive rather than gentle. At one point, a man had one of the spirit trumpets thrown at him while a woman was hit in the face by the illuminated octopus toy. There were other phenomena – apparently there was music and an illuminated trumpet rose into the air close to Robin Foy.

It was around forty minutes into the seance when something inexplicable happened. Somehow the lights came on to reveal me standing in the middle of the room with the spirit trumpet seemingly in my hand above me. According to most reports, I looked stunned and confused and then staggered backwards in a totally dazed state. Some people heard me mention the name Daniel. According to one account I said: 'They have let me down, it's Daniel's fault.' To be honest, the whole scene must have been so chaotic and confusing that it's no wonder different versions of events emerged later.

I was rushed to a quiet room where I came round. I knew something had gone wrong immediately I opened my eyes. I could feel pain in my stomach area and felt a bruise forming around my solar plexus.

John was sitting alongside me and explained what had happened. My instant reaction was to blame the spirit guides. 'What went wrong?' I said. 'How the hell could they let that happen to me?'

'I don't know, Colin, but it's happened,' he said.

When I saw Robin later that evening he told me that many of the guests had left in disgust. Several of them were convinced that I had been exposed as a fraud. We were all nonplussed by what had happened. There were so many unanswered questions. How had the lights come on? Who had switched them on – was it a spirit or a member of the audience? And how had I managed to get out of the chair when I had been so securely fastened? At that point everyone was still too shaken by the incident to be able to provide any answers. There was one thing of which we were all certain, however: this was not going to look good to the outside world.

Driving back to London, John tried to reassure me that it would be all right, but I knew that it wouldn't. Sure enough the incident caused a major controversy. *Psychic News* ran a big story at the beginning of November: 'Noah's Ark Society Rocked by Fraud Allegations. Medium Caught Holding Trumpet.' The Society were forced to issue a statement in which, to his eternal credit, George Cranley defended me to the hilt.

George said that the Society wanted to 'state emphatically that, through previous experiments, experience and long association with this medium, genuine physical phenomena have been consistently demonstrated'. He made clear that I was as upset by the incident as everyone else and was helping them in the investigation. Until that was over I'd also agreed not to demonstrate at Scole or any other Society seminars. He also reminded everyone why physical mediumship was 'historically proved to be controversial, enigmatic and paradoxical'.

The psychic press carried the statement in full, but deep down I sensed the damage that had been done.

In the days and weeks that followed I was left to nurse a mixture of feelings. I knew I wasn't a fraud but I knew how it looked. But I really couldn't understand how it had happened. I was also confused by all the different accounts of what people had seen during the four or five seconds when the lights had come on.

It had been reported that I had the trumpet in my hand, but some said that was not what had happened.

They said that the trumpet had been in the air and had suddenly dropped into my hand when the lights went on. To be honest, no one knew what the truth was but we all agreed that I wouldn't demonstrate again until there had been a full investigation.

For the Ark Society there was a lot at stake. In response to all the rumours, George told the press in another statement:

> In order to avoid such difficulties the Spiritualist movement largely divorced itself from such mediumship fifty years ago to court respectability. This incident will not weaken the Society's function nor resolve to see this highly evidential and precious form of mediumship emerge once again and become available to all people. The spirit world has entrusted us with this work and in consequence the Ark will proceed through rough and smooth waters on its journey. We shall not shirk our responsibility.

It was decided that a couple of things would happen. First of all an engineer named Hylton Thompson was given the job of doing a technical examination and report. One of the most interesting things I learned about the events of that night was that the cable ties that I was bound by had been shattered. Thompson enlisted the help of a guy called Jim White, an expert in polymers at Newcastle University, to examine the broken ties. But between them they found that there was no real explanation for the breakage. If they had been simply cut, there would have been stretching of the polymer but there were no signs of that. Another possible explanation was that they could have been freeze-dried in dry ice in advance. But the investigators said there was no chemical residue to confirm that. Which eliminated that possibility.

When the question 'In your opinion, how could someone have achieved this breakage of three 300lb strain-bearing ties?' was put to the examiners, they said that the only conceivable way it could have been done was if the ties had been held tight in a vice-like device on to which a very heavy guillotine blade had been dropped. That was the only way you could do it. The only problem with that, of course, was that if the cables had been tied to someone's wrists and ankles that person would have had their hands and feet cut off.

In short, Hylton's conclusion was that although fraud could not be eliminated all evidence made it unlikely. The report exonerated me in the greater part and the Society put out a statement saying they had total faith in me.

But I wanted to know what had happened. I simply couldn't understand how Magnus and my other guides had let this happen. They were supposed to be protecting me, especially in a highly vulnerable situation like that.

*

It was decided that we would hold a special, private seance at our home circle. Some of the senior members of the Noah's Ark Society came along, including Robin Foy and George and John.

I went into a trance once more. At one point an entity called Daniel appeared – and did exactly the same as he did before. He just shattered the cable ties and flicked on the lights. Fortunately, I was in the presence of some very experienced and wise old heads in George and John, so they took time to talk to him. He claimed he despised and hated me. I was everything he detested, apparently. There was no real explanation for this, from him at least, so the seance members asked the guides present for more help.

It was established this boy-spirit Daniel was quite disturbed. After some very firm questioning from the committee, it emerged that he was what is known as a 'rescue' – a spirit that needs to be encouraged to move on. More importantly, they asked the guides who were present at the seance why the spirit world hadn't protected me. It had been the spirit world that had asked for the creation of the Noah's Ark Society, so why hadn't it done more to protect the work that it was doing? The answer they gave was telling. 'We warned him not to go there that night,' one guide said. 'We gave him a message, but he ignored it.'

When I came out of trance and talked to George and John after the seance, they explained all this to me. 'Of course,' I said to John. 'That nausea I felt on the way to Norfolk that day. I should have realised it was a warning.'

It taught me a huge lesson. I vowed never to ignore messages like that again.

The incident and the publicity it caused shattered my confidence for a while. This was still a time when the internet was in its infancy but even then there were a couple of sceptic websites that went to town on the whole thing, calling me a charlatan, a fraud – and worse.

It wasn't true, of course. And it wasn't fair, either.

It really upset me. John sat me down one day and said: 'Colin, this is the life of a professional medium, and I know you are not the sort of person to run away. It will be an accusation you will have to live with for the rest of your professional life. But if you stay out there, demonstrating the same high level of professional mediumship, people will judge you on what you do – not on some old allegation.'

He was right, of course. I knew I wasn't a fraud. And I knew I had so much to give people as a medium. I couldn't let this be the end of that part of my life. I had to fight on.

I was heavily into positive thinking at the time and a great believer in Nietzsche's famous mantra: what doesn't kill you makes you stronger. I knew that if I wanted to emerge from this stronger I had to turn this huge negative into a positive.

So I made some decisions. I had promised not to demonstrate publicly again with the Noah's Ark Society, but was still determined to carry on with my home circle in Hove. I would also do all I could to defend my name.

I got some support from the then editor of *Psychic News*, who offered me an interview to give my side of the story. He promised to maintain my anonymity, although by that point a lot of people in the psychic community knew very well that I was Lincoln. I used the interview to emphasise that I hadn't done anything deceptive or fraudulent. I also made the point that I was still, effectively, a fledgling medium. The bottom line was that I had been pushed into the limelight as a physical medium at a very young age. The people who had practised it in the past had all been very senior figures, elderly men often. I had been given far, far too much attention and put under too much pressure.

In the future, I said, I knew I had to be cautious and not push my development too fast. In other words, I had to go back to school.

Finally, I decided that I would use this experience in a positive way. By this time I was being asked to do lectures, public speaking and seminars, as well as my regular sessions in Brighton at The Mystic Rainbow. I took that negative experience and turned it into a positive. I began teaching others about the dangers of running before they could walk, of trying to force

their development rather than letting it happen naturally. Once or twice I even began using that phrase of
Ida's that I used to find so patronising: 'You need to
have some grey hairs.'

11 | Friends in Need

FORTUNATELY I had good friends to help get me back on track. George Cranley and John remained my most passionate defenders, although by now I had also become friendly with a wide range of people through my mediumship. Carol Hawkins and her husband Martyn, in particular, became huge allies during the difficult period following the Scole seance. Carol had seen me demonstrate with Leslie Flint and had the utmost faith in me and my abilities. She, like John, told me to keep at it and to keep taking my message to the public.

By this time Martyn and she had got their own shops in Dorking, in Horsham and Haywards Heath, specialising in Spiritualism and the psychic arts. The Dorking branch had a basement that was ideally suited for seances. We began to hold them there. They quickly took off, with people paying to come to the seances and a waiting list of people wanting to join us. We immediately began to build a reputation.

Carol and Martyn were mediums too and, as the popularity of the seances grew, we decided to join

forces and put on a mini-tour of theatres and Spiritualist venues in the south of England. The shows were
billed as 'Spirit Force' and we performed at venues in
Guildford, Crawley and Wimbledon, demonstrating
to audiences of two hundred to three hundred people.
For me, it was a huge learning curve. It gave me my
first taste of 'performing' and taught me a lot about
the stage craft and 'entertainment' aspect of mediumship, something I'd first seen, of course, when I'd
watched Doris Stokes on stage in Brighton as a teenager.
As an actress, Carol understood how to interact with an
audience very well.

With her guidance, I learned that there was a subtle
difference between demonstrating at a Spiritualist
church and doing so in front of a paying audience. I
learned that it wasn't just about getting the messages
to those for whom they were intended, I had to
involve everyone else in the audience so that they all
felt they had had an enjoyable and rewarding time.

One of the most memorable messages I delivered
during this phase was to a middle-aged man at a Spirit
Force demonstration in Wimbledon, I think it was. By
now I had learned to tune into the wide variety of
voices, visions and thoughts that came into my head
with a lot more clarity and control. As the message
took shape, I sensed that he was quite sceptical, which
was fine. I rather enjoyed the challenge of persuading
sceptics that there was more to life – and death – than
they imagined.

I'd connected with his father and was passing on some details that he recognised.

I saw, for instance, that he was looking to buy a new house. He was quite shocked at this.

'Well, yes, that's true,' he said.

But then I told him that I was being shown the name of a house, Green Acres. 'Does that mean anything to you?' I said.

'No, nothing,' he replied, looking a little pleased that I'd gone off the scent, as it were.

One of the things I remembered from Ida's circle was the importance of sticking to my guns and believing in what I was being told by the spirit world. Even if the recipient of the message was saying they didn't understand it, I had to believe in what I was saying.

'Are you sure?' I said.

'Absolutely,' he said. 'It is meaningless to me.'

'Well, it will mean something to you one day,' I said.

Again, he looked doubtful.

A couple of months later I got a phone call from Carol. She'd received a letter from this guy which he'd asked her to pass on to me. Since the Spirit Force show he had successfully found himself a new home, a nice country cottage. The place had needed a fair amount of restoration. In particular, he and his wife had decided that they were going to remove the copious amounts of ivy that had grown around the house over the years.

It was while he was clearing the ivy around the arch of the front door that he came across a plaque with the house's old name on it. He hadn't seen the name referred to on the legal documents so was surprised to see it there. As he hacked away the ivy and cleaned it up, he saw that it read 'Green Acres'.

One of the regular members of the circle was a man called Nick McGlynn. He was a very jolly, positive character and his energy was infectious. He came along regularly and was hugely supportive of me. Nick was impressed with what I was doing and told me that he never thought he'd have an experience to compare with that he'd had with Leslie Flint, who'd recently passed over.

Nick was married to a lovely lady called Marie. A couple of times he showed me a photograph of her. She looked like Shirley Bassey, a very attractive lady. Marie used to accompany him to Leslie's seances but was no longer well enough to travel. She was suffering from emphysema and other chronic illnesses. Nick always talked about how much she would have loved to come along.

'One day she'll make it,' I kept saying to him. And sure enough, she did.

One week Carol got a call from Nick quite late in the afternoon, asking if there was a spare seat for that evening's seance. By pure chance, or perhaps not, Carol had just had a cancellation and offered Nick the spare seat. He turned up a few hours later, as usual, in a jovial, chatty mood. And, also as usual, I went into a trance and was oblivious to what was happening until I came round just over an hour and a half later.

Carol and Nick untied me from the chair. Both were smiling warmly at each other as if something special had happened.

'What is it?' I asked them.

It was Nick who explained.

'Colin, Marie passed away this morning,' he said.

I was stunned. 'Oh Nick, I'm so sorry to hear that,' I said.

'It's all right, Colin. She'd been suffering a great deal and it was probably for the best.' He explained that he'd not told me or Carol about her passing before the seance in case it cast a cloud over proceedings. 'But it seems like it didn't because you brought her through to me tonight,' he smiled.

'Really,' I said, surprised. It was very, very rare for someone to make contact within hours of passing. An adjustment period of days or more often weeks is the norm.

I looked at Carol. She was close to tears, I could tell, but she nodded. She confirmed that, halfway through tonight's seance, Marie had come through, speaking via me in her own voice. She had told him that she had crossed over safely. Not only that, at one point she had come over and held his hand. It had, apparently, been an incredibly moving moment for everyone in the circle.

Nick gave me a huge hug at the end of the evening. He told me that what had begun as one of the saddest days of his life had ended as one of the most joyous. That meant the world to me, especially after what I'd been through in the previous months. I'd carried Leslie Flint's words about the duty of a medium with me everywhere in the past weeks and was determined that I would help people as much as I could, and hopefully aid my own rehabilitation in the process.

Nick was incredibly grateful and afterwards spread the word about what had happened in the media. He became a champion for my cause at a time when I really needed one. He wrote a long letter to *Psychic News* in which he explained how his wife had materialised at a seance led by me just a few hours after her passing. He praised me to the skies, comparing me to Leslie Flint and saying that I had the same compassionate gift.

He also went on the radio to talk about the experience, facing up to the sceptics who were only too willing to dismiss his claims as nonsense.

At one point someone had said to him: 'And how do you know it was your wife's voice?'

'I was married to her for forty years, I think I'd recognise her voice,' he said.

In the months and years to come he was as instrumental as anyone in me getting my confidence back.

*

Nick was one of the small group of people who were convinced that I should take up mediumship professionally. My friend Michael had been saying this for a long time. His mantra was: 'Do you want to remain a carpet salesman all your life?'

I had been resistant to it. But as my seances with Carol began to become more and more popular, for the first time, I began to see that it might actually be possible. Any hopes I had of achieving that were quickly dashed, however. For the second time in just a few years I fell ill again – this time, seriously.

A small number of events in my life have been so unexpected and so dramatic that I have come to the conclusion they must have somehow been pre-planned by the spirit world. Such an event happened when, in my mid thirties, I suffered a stroke.

The events that led to it began one December night when I was heading home from the Stone carpet company's Christmas party with my mother. Chris hadn't wanted to come with me so I'd asked her if she'd like to join me instead. She enjoyed a party and liked the Stone family. Neither of us had had a drink. My mother doesn't drink and I abstained because I was driving my father's Volvo.

We'd left the party and were driving up and out of Brighton across the Ditchling Beacon when we approached a crossroads. It was a notorious accident black spot so I deliberately slowed down, even though it was my right of way.

Unfortunately, the only other driver on the road at that moment didn't do the same thing. Out of the blue, from the road to my right, a car came ploughing into the side of me. It must have been travelling at close to 50 mph. All I can remember is the impact of the collision and the sensation of being jerked backwards at speed.

In the immediate aftermath of the collision I was dazed. My first instinct was to check on my mother. She was badly shaken but I could see she was breathing and there were no obvious signs of injury. The next thing I saw was a young girl, climbing out of the other car – and then running away.

I managed to get myself out of the car safely and went round to get my mother out. When I got her to the side of the road she just passed out.

The car had been badly damaged and the brakes no longer worked, so it had started to roll back down the slope. Fortunately, there was a cottage across the road and its occupants appeared, obviously having heard the noise. They were able to help me put a rock under the back wheels to stop the car rolling away. One of them told me that he'd seen the girl running away from the scene and into a pub a short distance up the road. He recognised the car and told me it was the girlfriend of the landlord's son.

Within minutes the police had arrived. The first officer to reach me told me that I'd been incredibly lucky that I'd been driving such a well constructed car. 'If you'd been in something other than a Volvo I dread to think what would have happened to you and your mother,' he said.

To my astonishment, his colleague asked me to take a breathalyser test. 'Me take a breathalyser?' I said angrily. 'What about the girl who did this and who ran off? She was the cause of all this. I haven't had a drop all night, she's obviously the one who's been drinking. One of the neighbours here saw her running into the pub up the road.'

I was told to leave the investigation to them and after I'd given a detailed report was allowed to go home. By now my father and brother had arrived after being telephoned by a police officer.

As is so often the case with this type of incident, it was only later the full impact hit me. The day after the accident, I was too wrapped up in trying to find out the identity of the other driver and making an insurance claim. I had effectively written off my dad's car, which, needless to say, hadn't gone down too well in the Fry household.

I knew I didn't feel quite right, there was a ringing in my head and I felt quite dizzy at times. But I ignored it. That turned out to be a big mistake. It was two days later that it happened.

It was a Sunday night and Chris and my mum had gone out to play bingo together, leaving me on my own. Our lodger, Richard, was the one who found me. He walked into the house to find me collapsed at the top of the stairs. I came around in hospital.

My mother and Chris rushed to the hospital together. I was put in a side ward while I waited to see a doctor for a full consultation. My mother got there ahead of them, took one look at me and said: 'He's had a stroke.' When she collared a passing nurse and told her this the nurse looked at my mother as if she was an idiot.

'No, no, he's a bit young for that, Mrs Fry,' the nurse said.

'Listen, young lady, I've been a nurse since before you were born. I'm telling you he's had a stroke,' my mother said.

She was absolutely right. A doctor was soon called in and he confirmed that I was paralysed in my right arm, leg and shoulder and down the right side of my face. I was immediately put on a ward and told I'd be kept there for observation for a few days. At one point they got very worried about me because I started having fits as well. I'd never suffered anything like that before. They were concerned that the accident had triggered a stroke and maybe somehow triggered epilepsy at the same time.

In all, I was kept in for observation for a week. I was told that my mobility had been impaired and that it might not fully return. I was also told then when I left hospital I would be disqualified from driving for a while because epileptics aren't allowed to drive.

I lay in bed in hospital, terrified. I was terrified I would lose my job with the Stones. Driving was a major part of my role: I had to be able to see clients for estimates. But I was even more terrified of being crippled or infirm in some way.

It was then that, a little reluctantly and uncertainly, I turned to the spirit world for help. To be honest, I'd been surprised not to have been given a warning in advance. I'd had instances before where I'd been given a sign or a direct message telling me to avoid certain roads or places while out driving. One, in particular, when I was driving back from Lewes to home, had helped me avoid a terrible car smash in which a couple of people had been killed.

As I lay there in my hospital bed, I wondered why the warning hadn't come this time. I put the thought out to the spirit world, asking them whether I had anything to worry about. I got back nothing more than a message saying, 'We'd have told you if it was going to be serious.' But with the doctors now talking about me being permanently immobilised, I needed more than that. I needed help. I got it.

Slowly but surely, I began to recover. The diagnoses I received from the doctors were often confusing and contradictory, but the long-term prognosis was that I'd always have some limitation with the movement in my hands and maybe even my legs. I didn't want that to happen and was determined to walk again. So I'd actually started walking in the hospital at night after they'd told me I might be immobilised. I continued to rehabilitate myself at home after being discharged.

From then on, my health began to improve. I had to go for regular check-ups and doctors were soon noticing an amazing change. Earlier than expected, I got my driving licence back because they decided it couldn't be epilepsy. The Stone family had been really good to me and allowed me to keep working without driving, but I was relieved to get back on the road. On top of this, the seizures began to subside. From the expressions I was seeing on the doctors' faces when they looked at my results, it was clear that something was happening that was beyond their understanding. A few months after the stroke, I was told that they were hopeful I'd make a full recovery.

The doctor whom I saw regularly said he'd rarely seen such a strong rally after a stroke. Even more unusually, the brain scans which had previously shown an area of scar tissue had started to show the dark patch of damaged brain disappearing slowly but surely. Scar tissue doesn't usually disappear like that; it should remain for life. Yet mine vanished, as if it had never been there. When I asked one doctor about this, he said there was no explanation for it. Eventually, the doctors told me to forget about my regular six-month examinations. I was given a clean bill of health.

The only time I am reminded of how ill I was now is if I'm excessively tired. People who know me well tell me that the side of my face drops down slightly. But to all intents and purposes I bounced back from the accident as fit and strong as I'd been beforehand.

*

At first I had no real understanding of what this episode might mean. I knew that much of what happened to me happened for a reason, but there was no obvious explanation for this. It soon began to make sense, however.

A couple of months after I'd left hospital and returned to work, I began doing personal sittings again. I was visited one day by a lady who asked me whether I did healing clinics. I said that I did. I was a great believer in what the late, great medium Harry Edwards called 'the forgotten mediumship'.

'Can I send my husband to you?' she asked. 'He's had a stroke. And he's struggling. The doctors have told him that the only thing that's holding him back is himself.'

I agreed. The following week her husband came to see me at the temporary healing room I'd set up in one of the rooms of my house. He didn't look too happy to be there. The after-effects of the stroke were clear to see. He was still limping and walked with the aid of a walking stick. There was a slight droopiness to the left side of his face and his speech was a little drawled. But otherwise, he looked in good health.

He told me that he was in his early forties but had given up on getting another job. 'I'm a cripple, on the scrapheap,' he said.

His wife had been right: he was holding himself back. I didn't tell him this immediately. Instead I focussed on relaxing him and trying to use the healing energy to help him at least feel a little less depressed.

On a later visit, however, I suggested that he should be a more positive. 'It's easy for you to say that,' he said, quite angrily. 'You don't know what it's like.'

I knew the anger had to come out and was glad that it had. I just leaned forward and said to him: 'As a matter of fact I do. I had a stroke myself about the same time as you.'

I then explained to him what had happened to me. He was shocked. 'How come you are normal and I'm not?' he said.

I explained to him that I'd refused to give in to it – and that he should do the same.

Over the following weeks, I saw him several more times. I would lay my hands on him for spirit healing and we would chat about the progress he was making. And there was plenty of progress to talk about.

When I first met him he was very low and convinced that he would never work again, despite being a relatively young guy. Within a month or so, however, his manner had changed completely. He looked more positive and healthier, the droop in his face was less pronounced and he walked more freely than previously.

One day, after I'd applied some healing, I offered him a cup of tea.

'Sorry, got to get off early today. Got an interview for a job,' he said.

I was delighted. 'What is it?' I asked.

'Just a part-time job in a warehouse, sitting behind a computer probably, but I don't care,' he smiled.

'Good luck with that,' I said, inwardly delighted at his news.

The following week I got a phone call from him telling me that he'd have to stop the healing visits because he'd got the job. 'And they want me full time,' he said.

It was when I put the phone down to him that it struck me. There had been a reason why I hadn't been warned about that car on Ditchling Beacon. There was a reason why I'd had that stroke. To be an effective medium and healer I needed to experience things myself to understand them properly. It wasn't just that man who benefited from that experience. In the years that have followed, I've conveyed messages from stroke victims that have passed over to the other side as well as helped those on this side who have needed help with their rehabilitation. Each time I have done so I have felt their pain, literally.

12 | The Spirit Lodge

As I entered my mid-thirties I had a good life. I had a well paid job, a long-term partner, a loving family and a collection of good friends. By all conventional standards, I had all I needed to be content. And yet I wasn't. There was an itch that needed scratching.

Mediumship was still something that I did during the weekend or on a spare evening during the week. It wasn't at the centre of my life. Deep down, however, I had a strong feeling that it should be, that I should be doing more with my gift. It wasn't my *raison d'être*, but I felt it should be.

If there was one person who understood this more than any other it was Michael. My partner Chris was, to be honest, sceptical about what I did. My parents were more supportive, in particular my mother, and Nick McGlynn and Carol Hawkins remained encouraging allies. But Michael was the one who really had faith in me. Ever since we'd first met he'd say encouraging things about my work. He was convinced that there was something different about me and that something important and life-changing was going to happen.

And then, around 1995, something did happen – Michael had been diagnosed as being HIV positive a few years earlier, but took a turn for the worse that year. It proved to be perhaps the biggest turning point in my life. Seeing someone you love deteriorate through a terminal illness is an horrific experience. Michael had always been such an exuberant, positive person. Watching him slowly lose that spark and energy was heartbreaking for me.

His illness was manageable for a while but by 1997 he had begun to deteriorate. This meant that he needed a great deal of daily care. I devoted as much of my time as I possibly could to helping him. It wasn't easy, in fact it was downright hard work at times.

He needed bathing one day, so I gave him a bath. He slipped in the bath and I caught him to stop him falling. Now Michael was quite a big guy, he was about six foot tall and quite heavy. The medication he was on meant he had ballooned in weight. As I caught him and held on to his full weight, I felt my back go. I went to the osteopath and was told that I had ruptured a disc. I couldn't afford to take any time off work, as I was still at the carpet store by day and practising my mediumship by night. I was in absolute agony most of the time, although – interestingly – I discovered that the pain was much less severe when I was communicating with the spirit world during demonstrations at Spiritualist churches or elsewhere.

I had little time to dwell on this, however.

Michael's condition worsened in the autumn of 1997. He underwent combination therapy, which, at the time, was in its early stages of development. Today, of course, it allows people with HIV to lead a healthy and normal life but it was experimental at that time. Unfortunately, he sustained damage to his cardiovascular system because of the treatment. Slowly but surely his heart began to fail. With the hospital that had been treating him in Brighton unable to help, he was admitted to Kings College Hospital in London.

I went through a phase where I visited him there several times a week. By now he knew that his time was limited, so we spent those days together with my sitting by his bedside to talk about what would happen when he passed over.

'Come on then, tell me what you are going to do when I'm no longer here to look after you?' he said once, knowing it would make me cry. He came out with that old line that he had been trotting out for years. 'Are you going to carry on being a successful carpet salesman? Or are you going to be brave, are you going to make a difference to people's lives instead?'

We'd had this discussion many times. I was convinced there was no way I could make the same kind of living I was making in management. It just didn't add up. We were still in the 1990s. The era of Doris

Stokes had gone. Mediumship was very much confined to the Spiritualist community where new names like myself, Tony Stockwell and Gordon Smith were gaining a reputation to match those of established ones such as Glyn Edwards and Robin Stevens, who had been working in the churches and psychic centres for many years. Beyond that, however, there was only the 0800 numbers at the back of the newspapers. Phone 'Psychic Zelda': I wanted nothing to do with that.

But Michael was insistent. 'If you are meant to you will,' he said to me. 'Things will work out for you, I'm sure.'

By November 1997, his illness had taken an even more terrible toll on him physically. As his faculties began to fail, I took on more and more responsibility. I became his next of kin, legally – and from that point regarded him as my adoptive brother in every sense.

I had promised him I would be with him at the end, and I was. The last fun moment we shared came when I arrived at his bedside one evening, having dashed up from Brighton to London after work. I was exhausted but arrived to be told that Michael was insisting that I shave his chest. 'He won't let me do it,' said the nurse. 'The only person who is allowed to do it is you, apparently.'

So I had to use a razor and some shaving foam to shave Michael's very hairy chest. It was the last thing I wanted to do after a long day but it actually proved to be the source of a lot of laughs between the two of us. And it was the last time we laughed together. Michael died that month, November 1997. At this point I need to acknowledge my friend Vince, who did so much to help me with Michael's day-to-day care.

The minute Michael took his last breath I took the decision. I decided there and then that he was right. I wasn't going to spend the rest of my life managing a carpet shop. I was going to try to make a difference. I was going to honour Michael's memory by giving it a go as a professional medium.

First, however, I had to go through the process of grief like everyone else. I conducted Michael's funeral service myself with the help of a local vicar. Michael had made one very strange request. He wanted to be buried, which was a challenge at the time because of the terrible prejudice against HIV. But Michael made me promise there would be no gravestone on his grave. 'Memories should live in the heart and not on a piece of stone,' he said. As the years have gone by I've come to realise that this was one of the wisest things I think I've ever heard.

I dealt with all his affairs. I had been given power of attorney to deal with his estate after he passed. But when all that was sorted, I basically took the plunge. I chucked in my job and walked away. It was, looking back on it, a crazy, rash thing to do. For a start, I had just taken on a fairly hefty mortgage, which I had to pay each month. But from the beginning it just seemed to work out for the best. Just like Michael said it would.

Within days of Michael's funeral I got an invitation to visit Australia. The trip had been organised by George Cranley, who had received an invitation to demonstrate there and promised there would be opportunities for me too. George and I booked tickets for ourselves and a third person, Vince Cross, a guy I'd befriended at my awareness group at The Mystic Rainbow. Vince was someone I had taken an instant liking to. He had this vibrancy and excitement about him. In many ways, he was like Michael. I became very close to him and he moved in with Chris and myself. Soon after that he volunteered to become my manager.

I thought it was a great idea. I was beginning to travel so much, I needed a companion, organiser, sounding board.

With Vince's encouragement, George made contact with some Spiritualist organisations in Australia and arranged for me to do a series of seances, lectures and sittings in Melbourne and Adelaide. I was still grieving for Michael, but at the same time a part of me was excited at this new departure.

All was far from plain sailing, however. The day before I was supposed to fly I did my back in again. I hadn't quite recovered from the damage I'd caused catching Michael in the bath months earlier. I went to see a chiropractor and he said there was no way I could fly the next day.

I just looked at him. 'I have no choice, I have to go. I have a month of work arranged out there,' I said.

He sat there and looked at me for a while. Then he said: 'The only way you can travel is if I inject steroids straight into your spine.'

'OK,' I said, not even thinking about what that might mean.

A short time later, the chiropractor led me to a bed where there was some equipment ready. 'You are going to have to lie on this bed, and you can scream and shout as much as you like – and swear, but you must not move,' he said.

I have to say it was the most agonising experience that I've ever had in my life.

But I got on the plane and I got to Australia.

The trip had been organised by a couple called Garth and Audrey Wiley who ran a centre on the outskirts of Melbourne called the Woodlands Spiritualist Sanctuary. It was a fantastic place, set in beautiful, isolated countryside overlooking a nearby range of mountains. It was while I was out there that I sensed Michael with me for the first time. I would feel him around me several times in the months and years to come, but to feel him close at this time was especially moving for me.

My mediumship had now developed to such an extent that I could get messages in all sorts of ways. Often I would see or hear people talking directly to me. At other times, however, a simple thought, word or phrase would suddenly appear in my head without any explanation whatsoever. It was while I was sitting in the gardens at Woodlands one evening, watching the blood-red sun go down, that I found myself thinking a simple phrase: 'You might think you've come far – but there's still a long way to go.' I'm convinced that it was Michael's spirit, encouraging me on as ever.

Michael's advice for me to turn professional looked more and more astute as the months went by. I came back from Australia to find my diary filling up with invitations to give seminars, seances and lectures. When I'd taken that leap of faith and quit my job, I'd put the thought out to the spirit world that, if they wanted me to do their work, then they needed to look after me. During those early days of my mediumship – and indeed ever since – there was always just enough. Just enough meetings, just enough sittings, just enough seminars, just enough to pay the bills and pay the mortgage. And it was the same thing whenever I got an unexpected bill: I'd get a phone call asking me to come and do a demonstration here or a lecture there. It was uncanny. Something always seemed to come up just in time.

One day in 1999 I got a phone call from Nick McGlynn, asking whether he could pop over to see me at home. Nick had been such a supportive and inspirational friend in recent months. After a long wait, I had at last gone into hospital for a major back operation to correct the damage done to my discs. It was supposed to have put me out of action for three months but only a few days after I came out of hospital I was working again. Unfortunately, I couldn't drive for any length of time and one night I had a booking for clairvoyant demonstration all the way down in Axminster in Devon. Vince didn't drive and Chris had something on as well. In a panic I rang Nick. Amazingly he offered to drive me down there in his car. I lay in the reclined front seat, flat on my back all the way to Devon and back.

I assumed Nick wanted to see me on this particular morning for a sitting, which I was always happy to give him. But to my surprise he wanted to talk about something else.

During that long drive down to Axminster, and on other occasions as well, Nick and I talked a lot about the way my career was going. He knew that I was finding it a strain to keep running the seances with Carol and Martyn, while the demand for those seances was enormous. We had a six-month waiting list. I'd also begun doing private sittings and healing clinics for people, but had either been using my house, which wasn't ideal, or hiring rooms in hotels. I'd also used a place called Jenny's Sanctuary in Banbury, but the process of travelling to lots of different venues had become a bit of a pain, to be honest.

'Colin, I know you are going to say no, but can I make a suggestion?' Nick said as we both sat down with a cup of coffee in the kitchen.

I gave him a sheepish look and just said, 'Go on.'

'You've got all that space at the bottom of your garden. Why don't you build your own personal centre there? All you need is enough space to hold a maximum of say a couple of dozen people in a seance. You could then do sittings, healing clinics, seances – everything – down there,' he said.

I instantly saw what he meant. My garden was a decent size and there was a large area of space at the bottom. But it was a non-starter financially at that stage. 'Nick, it's a great idea but I simply don't have the money to do it,' I said.

'Ah,' he said, 'that's where I come in. I'll pay for it.'

I was slightly taken aback. 'No, Nick, I couldn't possibly let you do that,' I said.

He just looked at me and smiled. 'It's not a choice. I'm telling you that's what we're going to do. I have got more money than I need and this is what Maria would have wanted me to do with it,' he said. 'So let's have no more arguments about it. Start designing it and we will build it.'

And so it was that I began work designing what I immediately decided to call The Spirit Lodge. Nick and I looked around and came up with a plan to build a large, wooden building that would be double-glazed, soundproofed and totally insulated. The main floor space was around 21 feet by 10 feet, not huge, but more than enough space for my purposes.

From the moment I opened it for business that year, it transformed my fortunes.

I'd been really grateful to Carol and Martyn, but I decided to hold my monthly seances in the Lodge from now on. I immediately had a strong following and soon had to start running a waiting list. I also conducted spiritual healing clinics, small talks and seminars and, most of all, private one-to-one sittings.

My finances saw a huge improvement. For the first time ever, I was making money out of my mediumship. It felt great. To my delight, I was soon asked to write a weekly column in *Psychic News*, which did wonders to help publicise and spread awareness about the Lodge. Around this time also I was invited to join *Psychic News'* annual Spiritualist Symposium, something I continued with throughout the late 1990s when it was taken over by *Two Worlds* magazine.

The Spirit Lodge grew steadily into a success, not just from a business point of view, but from a psychic one too. It had a great atmosphere and warmth. From the beginning it produced memorable messages, not just for my clients and those who attended the seances and seminars I ran there – but for me and my family as well.

My family, both the living and the dead, has always been at the centre of my psychic life. My mother's parents were, as I've described, the most important influences in my early development. Between them they taught me that life does go on after death, and that the spirits of those who have passed over are always close by, watching over us and, if necessary, ready to help us. But other relatives have appeared to me in various forms over the years. Each and every one of them has taught me something.

As The Spirit Lodge began to establish itself, I worked with a range of other mediums and psychics, representing the whole range of abilities. One of them was a psychic artist, called Jan Dayton. (A psychic artist is someone who communicates the thoughts and energies they are picking up in a visual way.) We were running a workshop one Sunday when Jan began drawing an elderly man. As the picture began to take shape I realised that I recognised him. It was my great-uncle Charles.

Charles was my grandmother's brother, one of the nine children thrown to the four winds after my great-grandmother Minnie Carter committed suicide. He had played an important role in freeing my gran from the asylum to which she'd been committed. Charles's own marriage was a happy one, although it was laced with sadness. Charles had actually been married before he married my great-aunt Vera. When he and Vera fell in love, Charles had sought a divorce. But his first wife had refused to grant it for years. For many years Vera and Charles lived together as a married couple, with my great-aunt even changing her surname to his, even though she wasn't married. Eventually, after a long and bitter fight, Charles was able to dissolve the marriage and marry the love of his life. But then, not long after they got married, he contracted Parkinson's disease. His later years were difficult and demanding, especially for Vera, who became his nursemaid.

It was a cruel twist of fate. Vera had married Charles hoping to enjoy being legally wed after all those years of secrecy and subterfuge. Instead she'd acquired a patient who needed looking after. I have often thought that my great-aunt Vera, who we were all terribly fond of, must have felt that the illness had cheated her. I remember discovering the truth about their marriage when once I innocently asked Charles how long they'd been married. He'd said ten years but I'd put it down to his Parkinson's. Another aunt had explained the story to me.

When Charles died, Vera in her grief moved to Canada with her sister, where she had other family. I think she hoped to find happiness there but sadly she spent the last days of her life in a nursing home with dementia. She passed a couple of years before I set up the Lodge.

I was reminded of all this when I saw the drawing of my great-uncle. When I showed the picture to my mother, who had decided to join us at the workshop, we were both struck by how Jan's drawing was an absolute likeness of a photograph we had of Charles with Vera.

When everybody had gone home and we talked, we concluded that, as Vera had recently passed over, this was Charles's way of saying that they were happy together on the other side, where they had been freed from the physical shackles that had blighted their life here.

My mother found it a particularly moving message, one of many she received during that time. She was still a regular visitor to the house and would often pop in, usually unannounced, for a cup of tea and a chat. By now it was clear that I was finally 'going somewhere' with my mediumship, and she had become increasingly interested in my work. Her friendship with Pat remained and when I opened The Spirit Lodge they began to join me for the occasional evening seance or a workshop.

It was at one of these seances that my mother received a message that I will never forget. As usual, I'd gone into a trance and re-emerged a couple of hours later to hear what had happened. Everyone, except my mother, had explained what they had heard and what they felt it meant to them. But when it came to my mother's turn, she told me that she'd prefer to talk to me in private. So when everyone else had gone home, we made a cup of tea and chatted in the kitchen.

'What did you get, who was it?' I asked her.

'Jackie,' she said.

I was nonplussed. 'Who's Jackie?'

'You never knew this, but before I had Glenn, I was pregnant with a little girl who we were going to call Jackie,' she said. 'But I miscarried her.'

'I knew you lost a baby girl,' I said, to her astonishment. 'I remember it well. What I didn't know was that you and dad were going to call her Jackie.' My mother and I had never discussed it, but the memory had never left me.

My mother shook her head in disbelief as I recalled in vivid detail how I'd discovered her on the bathroom floor with blood all around her and had run to Auntie Cathy next door.

'Colin, I never knew you'd understood what had happened,' she said.

'I did, of course I did,' I said. 'It meant so much to me because I always wanted a sister,' I told her. 'That's why I was so mean to Glenn when I was little.'

By now Mum was dabbing at her eyes with a handkerchief. We chatted long into the night, in a way that we hadn't done since my teenage years. It was one of those conversations that mothers and sons have only once or twice in their lives.

If I'd shut down The Spirit Lodge that night and never used it again, it had more than justified its existence. But, of course, I didn't and that was only the first of many significant moments I experienced in that little makeshift centre at the bottom of my garden.

13 | The Vigil

O<small>NE</small> morning in the summer of 2000, I got a phone call from my father. When I heard him speaking in a very agitated voice, which was very much unlike him, I knew that something serious must have happened. 'Colin, I'm taking your mother to the hospital,' he said. 'She's been vomiting black blood and she keeps losing consciousness. I don't know what's wrong with her.'

I felt like someone had punched me in the stomach with incredible force, but knew I had to keep it together and not sound too panic-stricken. 'OK, Dad, I'll see you at the hospital. I'll drive straight there now,' I said. I got showered and dressed as fast as I could and headed to the hospital in Haywards Heath.

My mother hadn't been in the best of health in recent years. She had taken early retirement because she was suffering from a condition called polymyalgia rheumatica which had caused muscle wasting. She also suffered from diabetes. She was on medication for her illnesses, however, so I had no idea what had caused her to become so ill that she needed to be hospitalised.

By the time I got there my dad and my brother were already sitting in a waiting area, looking terribly worried. My mum's best friend Middy was also there. My dad was too distraught to speak, as was my brother, so I took Middy to one side and asked her what had happened. She explained that my mother had been rapidly taken from the A&E department to Intensive Care, where she was now on life support.

We all sat there in silence for a few minutes, each of us lost in our thoughts. I chatted a little to Middy but my dad wasn't able to speak, he was in pieces. I had never seen him in such a vulnerable state.

It wasn't long before a doctor appeared. Thanks to an amazing bit of good luck, we had a New Zealander consultant who was covering in casualty as a doctor that day. 'We should know more within a couple of hours,' he said, reassuring us that they were doing all they could to make her comfortable.

We'd been there another hour or two when another consultant appeared. This one had a very different air about him; he was quite arrogant. The news he had for us was shocking in the extreme. 'Your mother has a serious problem with her kidneys. They are basically failing and she has gone into toxic shock. We have got her on life support, but I don't think there's a lot of point in it. So I'm seeking your permission to switch the life support off.'

It was so sudden and absolute, delivered like a fait accompli. My dad just stood there, devastated, as if his entire world had fallen in, which it had in a way. My brother was close to tears, as was Middy, who was focussing on comforting both men.

I'd already starting picking up an energy on the way to the hospital and knew the spirits were close at hand ready to guide me. I knew instantly what I had to say and that I had to take the lead in dealing with this. 'Categorically no,' I said. 'My mother is going to recover from this, I know she is.'

The consultant looked at me as if to say, 'Who are you and how do you claim to know this?' Fortunately he didn't ask me this directly, otherwise I would have had to tell him that I was a Spiritualist medium and I was getting clear guidance from the afterlife that my mother's life was not about to come to an end.

'No, I agree with my son,' my father said, drawing another arch of an eyebrow from the consultant. I could tell that he was going to argue the case with us but, fortunately, before it turned into a major argument, the other consultant, whom we'd seen earlier, arrived.

He asked to have a word with his colleague. The two had a brief confab during which I could tell the first consultant was getting irritated. 'It's Friday, we have her in ICU. She is on life support, it won't cost anything to keep her on it over the weekend,' the New Zealander then said in earshot of all of us.

'I suppose so,' the other consultant said, before storming off.

The New Zealander then came to us to give us the news that my mother had been given a reprieve and had the weekend to show signs of recovery.

With the pressure off a little I told my dad and brother to go home. By then my dad's eldest brother, David, had turned up, so I got him to take them back in his car. 'I'll stay with Mum,' I assured them. 'One of you can relieve me later on tonight.' I had done it deliberately: I wanted to be on my own with her.

I was shocked when I went into the room. The sight of a close relative seriously ill in hospital is always shocking, but to see my mother in this condition was really upsetting. She was in a coma and was attached to a very sophisticated machine that was keeping her blood clean now that her kidneys had stopped functioning. My natural instinct was to burst out crying. But I knew that I had to be strong not just for her but for the whole family. I needed to work out what to do here.

All my years as a medium and a healer came together in the next few hours and days. I drew on everything that I'd learned since I was a boy.

I took the decision that I was either going to get her out of this situation, or – if that was not possible – then I was going to see her safely across to the other side. If it was her time, it was her time.

Somehow, however, I knew that it wasn't – and I knew that for one very good reason.

Throughout that morning I hadn't heard the voice telling me 'not long'. The spirit that I believed to be Minnie Carter (my mother's grandmother) had not come through to me.

I knew she was still present because I'd heard her only recently, when I visited another elderly friend in a hospital. But during those long, anxious hours in the hospital, she was completely absent. That gave me a huge boost. I felt certain that my mother wasn't meant to pass over at this point in her life.

My mother was sixty years old and had struggled a lot with her health. But equally I knew that she was a fighter, that she'd come through everything else that had been thrown at her. She had come through all her back troubles and even a bout of spinal meningitis. I knew she had the capacity to fight her way back to fitness. I had to help her as much as I could.

As I sat there with my mother, listening to the noise of the ventilator pumping away quietly and the beeping of the machine measuring her heart rate, a nurse came in. She was a lovely, chatty individual.

We started talking about the machine. 'How many do you have?' I asked.

'Just this one, and it had just become free when your mum arrived,' she said.

'What if it hadn't?' I said.

She just gave me a little shake of the head. 'If this machine hadn't been available, your mum wouldn't be here,' she said. This again reinforced my conviction that it was not time for my mum to pass over.

Over the course of the next forty-eight hours, my brother, Dad and I took it in shifts to be with Mum. During the periods I was there, I applied my healing skills and talked to my mum. Dad was in a bad way, unsure what to do with himself. After he left to go home on the second evening, I spoke quietly to my mother. According to the nurse, she was in such a deep coma that she couldn't hear anyone, but I just had a feeling she would listen to me.

'I know you can hear me and you can't respond. If you have to go then you have to go, but Dad needs you and that means you have to fight,' I said, holding her hand tightly.

On Sunday the New Zealander consultant came back in. He was supposed to be off duty but he came in to see her in any case. 'You must get some sleep,' he told me.

'I will do when I know she is better,' I said.

We then sat down and chatted about what treatment they were going to give her and what signs we needed to be looking for if she was to make a recovery.

'Are you medically qualified? You're using some very technical medical terms,' he said to me at one stage.

'I'm a registered spiritual healer and have people who help me,' I smiled. I'm pretty sure he didn't have a clue what I meant by the latter part of that.

Throughout this time I basically had spirits telling me what was happening.

At one point, a pair of nurses came in to adjust the humidity on the ventilator. I saw that they had turned it down and received an instant message that this was wrong. 'No, you have to increase it, not decrease it. In cases like this you need to increase humidity if you want to revive the kidney function,' I said, somehow developing a detailed medical knowledge. The nurses consulted with each other and went away. A few minutes later one of them returned, looking a little sheepish. She then turned the humidity up.

As the hours passed, doctors and nurses kept coming in. One of the nurses there was someone I'd known since the 1980s, when he had been a member of the same gay group as me. Because he knew me and my family he came over to see me. He knew I was a medium and asked me whether I'd got any guidance. I explained to him what I was hearing and he just nodded.

'So you don't think I'm some phoney then,' I said, pleased to be able to talk to someone I knew.

'Not at all,' he said. 'Every doctor and nurse has seen things that they can't explain logically. The human spirit is a mysterious and amazing thing.'

As the weekend drew to a close I began to get a clear picture from the spirit world of what was going to happen. I sensed that she would be in here for twenty days or so but that she would turn a corner on Monday and come out of her coma after that. When I said this to the medical team during their rounds on the Sunday night they just looked at me as if I was slightly mad. By Monday, however, her vital signs were showing signs of improvement. She was on her way back. Everything I was saying was happening.

Soon the other families in intensive care were beginning to take an interest in what was going on. One of them asked me to come and sit with her father for a while, which I agreed to do. They were incredibly grateful.

By the middle of the week, all the signs were that my mother was going to pull through. Her body was healing itself. It was going to be a long road to recovery but she'd get there. Three weeks later she was given the all clear and was able to come home. It was not the only healing that occurred that week . . .

Times of crisis test families to the limit. They either pull together or are pushed apart. In our case, it brought us closer. Relations between me and my brother and father hadn't been great in recent years. My brother and I had fallen out and my father had remained disapproving of what he would call my 'lifestyle'. But during those seemingly endless hours in the waiting rooms and cafe of the hospital I was able to make my peace with both of them.

My brother and I talked and discovered that we'd fallen out over what was really a misunderstanding. I don't feel that my brother and I will ever be close, but then maybe in families you don't always have to like the people you have to love!

The most poignant talk I had, however, was with my father. I had only seen my dad cry twice in my life. The first time was when his brother died and the second was when my mum was ill. To see my dad totally desolate like that had a profound effect on me. I had never seen him so vulnerable, and I never want to see him in that state again. The thought of losing my mother was simply too much for him to bear. They had been married at this point for thirty-nine years. I would be hard-pressed to find a couple who loved each other as much after all that time as they did when they first met. If not more. But they did.

One evening the two of us were sitting alone in the family room on the ward. He was staring into another cup of coffee, lost in his thoughts. I'd sensed that our time sitting here in the hospital had strengthened our relationship, so summoned the strength to say something that I'd wanted to say for many years.

'I know that it's always been hard for you to understand this life I lead as a gay man,' I said to him. 'And I know that by coming out I must have been a great disappointment to you . . .'

He didn't respond.

'. . . but I hope I have been a good son, Dad.'

Dad wasn't one for talking too much. He came from that generation that doesn't wear its emotions on its sleeve. But he just raised his head, gave me a long, slow smile and said: 'Why would you think otherwise?'

During those three weeks I'd had to switch off my emotions. It was ironic – the most emotional member of the family had been forced to keep it together and not go to pieces. I'd had to be there for them. At that particular moment, however, I cracked just a little bit.

My career as a professional medium was continuing to go well at this point. After visiting Australia for the first time, I'd been invited back there twice. I'd gone with Vince the first couple of times but on the third occasion, in 2001, I took Nick McGlynn with me. In addition to this I'd been invited to Japan to mark the 100th anniversary of the Japanese Spiritualist Society. The most significant overseas work I'd done, however, was a little closer to home, in Sweden.

I had received an invitation to visit the town of Ramsberg, home of the famous Ramsbergsgarden Spiritual Centre. I'd heard a little bit about the place during a previous trip to lecture in Finland. The Ramsbergsgarden had been founded in the 1960s and was regarded as the home of the Swedish Spiritualist movement.

I was bowled over by the place and the people imme-diately. Set in beautiful, peaceful Swedish countryside, the centre was a large, rather ramshackle, wooden build-ing in the traditional Scandinavian style. What it lacked in facilities it more than made up for in energy, charm and pure spiritual peace. I felt instantly at home and, after a successful first visit, went back there again a few months later.

There was something about the place that immediately connected with me. Part of it was the natural beauty of the place. There was something magical about it, particularly in the summertime when the sun would stay up in the sky until late in the night. I sensed a very strong energy from the spirit world telling me that this was a place that would play an important part in my future. And so it proved, in more ways than one.

My 'bread and butter' remained the classes, seances and one-to-one sittings that I did at The Spirit Lodge. By now I was receiving more and more visitors. My name was really spreading across the UK. I found I was constantly learning. One of the key lessons was that I couldn't edit what the spirit world was telling me. I had to tell the truth, and nothing but the truth.

A good example of this came when I did a sitting for a mother, I'll call her Abigail, who arrived with a gold signet ring she wanted me to hold while I did the reading. We call this branch of mediumship psychometry, the gift for getting information from the spirit world via a physical object. It was, for me, at least, an unreliable way of getting messages. I had often failed to gain anything from an object. But on this occasion I got a clear image immediately.

'The boy who owned this ring worked in a brick-works,' I said. Abigail nodded.

I got the very strong feeling that he was her son – and that he had passed over quite recently. I also felt that Abigail had been struggling to come to terms with his passing. I also picked up the boy's name, Jimmy or James. It was then that I began to sense that he had taken his own life, although it wasn't the usual kind of energy I got with a suicide. This seemed to me to be a possible explanation for Abigail's suffering, although we didn't go into that.

Abigail was pleased with the sitting and asked to bring her husband back for another sitting at The Spirit Lodge. I said yes. Part of my job is to help lift the burden of pain a great many people carry about those who have passed over. I felt there was more that Abigail needed to learn to help her deal with her situation.

She and her husband returned a couple of weeks later. I was able to connect with Jimmy again. This time I got a much clearer image of what had happened at the end of his life. And this was when my dilemma took shape. I saw, quite clearly, that Jimmy had died, not by committing suicide, but as the result of a sexual experiment that had gone badly wrong. He had tried hanging himself with a tie and accidentally choked himself to death. It was similar to the accidental death of the rock star Michael Hutchence. Jimmy's parents had clearly been suffering a great deal so I really didn't know whether I should tell them this detail.

'Jimmy is embarrassed about something,' I said to them.

'Tell him that it's all right,' his mother said. His father, who was very quiet throughout, nodded in agreement. 'Just tell us, we need to know,' he said.

'I know that people thought I tried to commit suicide but it's not true. The real story is that I accidentally hanged myself – I used to get a kick out of trying it,' Jimmy said through me.

I really wasn't sure what to expect when this came out. Part of me was expecting them to express shock or even anger. But instead they both let out an audible sigh of relief. It was as if an enormous weight had been lifted off their shoulders. 'We knew that was what had happened; we couldn't accept that he committed suicide but we just needed to hear it from him,' Abigail said.

This taught me a really important lesson, one that went to the very heart of my role as a medium: I was only the messenger; I shouldn't worry about what the message was.

The messages I was passing on were often extremely powerful, life-changing – and occasionally even life-saving – in their intensity. One morning I received a visit from a middle-aged lady. She was very agitated when she arrived and didn't calm down much when I gave her a cup of tea.

'Please don't be nervous,' I said, beginning the reading.

As I began to sense a series of images of a young boy in a wheelchair, I started to feel a real sense of nervousness myself. I could feel that this woman was on an emotional knife edge. Anything could happen, I sensed.

It was soon revealed that the boy was her son and he had been born with cystic fibrosis. From early on doctors had predicted that he would live a very short life. Yet despite this, his mother – and the rest of his family – had devoted themselves to caring for him. He had died in his sleep when he was thirteen. His mother had prepared herself for that day for a long time. But as I'd seen many times, there are some passings for which people simply can't prepare. They are too devastating. So it was with this lady's son.

The fact that I had connected with him changed her mood markedly. But I still felt she was in a highly volatile state. It was then that I got one of the most vivid and shocking messages I've ever received. Out of nowhere I had a vision of this woman throwing herself under a train. She was wearing exactly the same clothes as she was wearing sitting in front of me at that moment.

The truth dawned on me immediately: she was planning to take her own life today. She wanted to join her son on the other side and had prepared herself for that by making contact with him through me this morning.

It was then that her son came through with a clear message. 'You must not do what you are planning to do. It will not bring you closer to me,' he said.

When I told her this she got very upset and denied that she had any such plans. When I told her that I had seen an image of her throwing herself in front of a train, however, her demeanour changed completely. She broke into uncontrollable floods of tears. She told me that she had felt helpless and angry since her son had passed over. She simply didn't know what else to do.

I gave her another cup of tea to calm her down. Fortunately, her son's energy was still strong – he clearly had more to say to his poor, tortured mother. He explained what a wonderful thirteen years he had enjoyed on this earthly plane. He remembered in great detail family gatherings, parties and Christmases. He said that his family had given him a wonderful life and suggested that they had been very close because of his condition – and the knowledge that he might not live to an old age.

It was a remarkable message, one that I have recounted many times in interviews and in lectures around the world. It was remarkable because it illustrated the importance of living a natural life and of not breaking the natural order of things. As this lady's son had explained, by committing suicide and joining him too soon, she would have ruptured the natural order. She stayed with me for another half an hour or so, long after her session had officially ended. As she left she was much more composed and less agitated than when she'd arrived.

I must admit I was very worried about her. I was delighted when she contacted me again a few weeks later. She told me that she'd taken her son's message on board and started getting on with her life again.

'I'm doing what I should have done a long time ago,' she told me. 'Thank you for giving my son the chance to tell me that.'

I've received many powerful messages during my career. But I don't think I've ever received one to compare with that in its raw emotion and power.

14 | A New Dimension

IN late 2001, I was in Ramsberg teaching at the Ramsbergsgarden centre, when I got an email from a television producer asking me whether I'd be interested in doing a television series. Her name was Hilary Goldman from a company called IPM, based in London. She sounded very keen but it would be fair to say that I was underwhelmed. I'd been approached about going on television before and decided against it. I did so again this time.

There were a few reasons for this. Firstly, I was doing rather well as a performing medium in the UK. My public demonstrations at theatres and other venues were becoming popular. Vince and I had put on a few demonstrations at medium-sized halls around the south of England. I'd also taken part in some 'Mediumship' shows organised first by *Psychic News* and then *Two Worlds* magazine. They included other rising mediums like Tony Stockwell, Gordon Smith and Lynn G. DeSwart, and were mostly based around the London area. We went on stage in venues such as the Mermaid Theatre and the

Friends Meeting House. They were great fun and I learned a lot from them, not least that I always needed to wear a hearing aid on stage. My occasional deafness was still causing me problems.

I had also done other media work, including a radio programme with BBC Radio Four about the Noah's Ark Society and Noah Zerdin. I'd also made a series of DVDs about Magnus, my spirit guide, as well as some books with the former editor of *Psychic News*. As if all this wasn't keeping me busy enough, I was becoming extremely committed to the Ramsbergsgarden in Sweden, where I was now the senior tutor and Principal. I loved the place. The centre was struggling to stay in business and I wanted to do all I could to help it.

The main reason that I ignored the email, however, was that I really didn't trust television when it came to mediums. Mediums had always been given a rough time on television and had always been very restricted in what they were allowed to do on screen. The then-controlling body for British television, the ITC, had an unbelievably prejudiced attitude. We mediums were labelled under the all-encompassing banner of 'the occult', which for a Spiritualist is incredibly insulting because mediumship is an aspect of our religion. Indeed, Spiritualism is a recognised religion.

Over the years I'd seen a few documentaries in which Spiritualist organisations became involved and the impression I got was that the television companies had basically stitched them up. The programme makers had edited them in such a way as to put these 'flaky Spiritualists' on display. So taking all these things into consideration, I really didn't have any great desire to go on television and expose myself and what I do as a subject of ridicule. Just for public entertainment.

This particular producer wasn't easily put off, however. After receiving my 'thanks, but no thanks' email, Hilary Goldman wrote to me again – and again, explaining what she wanted to achieve. As I read her messages, I began to see that she might have a point. Perhaps the tide was finally turning in favour of mediums on television.

It was pointed out to me that the Liverpool-based medium Derek Acorah had been on Granada Breeze and done a TV series called *Psychic Livetime*. Perhaps more significantly, Living TV had started showing *Crossing Over* with an American medium called John Edward. But, in all honesty, I was so busy at the time, I didn't really watch much television. I was aware of Derek but I hadn't ever seen John Edward. I suggested that Hilary Goldman send me some DVDs so that I could see what approach was being taken. I watched John Edward and thought he was quite good. He seemed to be the first person who'd been allowed to do what a medium does, which is to convey messages to people in an audience from the afterlife.

I still wasn't convinced, however. I still thought of myself as a working Church, Spiritualist medium. I was well known within my community, doing what I wanted to do, and I didn't see any reason to change it. But when I said no again, Hilary called me directly. She explained that she'd like to propose a British version of *Crossing Over* with John Edward.

However, it was when she told me about how she'd found me that my ears pricked up. She told me that her cousin, a man called Michael de Vries, sat in one of my development circles. I knew Michael well. He had been part of my regular Friday-night group. I thought of him as a friend, and still do. That changed my attitude completely. If he trusted this lady, then she must be on the level.

So I agreed to meet her when I got back from Sweden. She came down to my house in Haywards Heath with a guy called Alan who, I was told, would be the producer if it got off the ground. It was a memorable meeting. I'd put together this long list of things that I was prepared to do and an even longer one of things I wouldn't do. I started reeling it off but was interrupted by Hilary: 'Hold on, I think you've got the wrong idea. I've come to you because of your reputation and the personal recommendation of people. If it's to work, this series has to be built around what you do,' she said.

I was hugely encouraged by this.

She went on to explain that it would be a mixture of me working with an audience theatre-style and then doing one-to-one sittings. I said that it was important that I never met the people that came into the studio and didn't want any prior warnings of those who were coming for the sittings. She agreed immediately.

Looking back I can see that I really was a bit paranoid about being made to look ridiculous. 'Please don't take offence, but if you do anything to ridicule me or make me feel bad I will walk away,' I said at one point. I was right to be cautious, of course, but fortunately I had found a person of integrity in Hilary, someone with whom I sensed I could form a really good working relationship.

At the end of that meeting it was agreed that I would drive up to Loughton in Essex, where Hilary lived, in order to film some material for a pilot. So on the agreed day I put on a jacket and tie and duly set off for Essex. Once there, I did a demonstration for some thirty people, arranged theatre-style. The most interesting – and amusing – message that came across concerned a man who received a message from his mother.

I identified him from an image of a uniform that his mother had put in my mind. It was dark blue and had a lot of silverware on it. It was clear he was a senior figure either in the Police or the Armed Forces. A guy in the audience connected with this and made himself known. As he wasn't on duty, he was in civvies and was sitting next to a rather glamorous younger woman.

The message intensified and I got the very strong impression that his mother wasn't happy with his behaviour when he was out of uniform. 'Your mother is telling me that what you are doing to your wife and to your son is wrong, and she really doesn't like to see you carrying on like that,' I told him.

He didn't say anything but I could see him – and the lady next to him – squirming uncomfortably in their seats. It was only later that Hilary revealed to me that the lady was his mistress and that he had been having a long-running affair behind his wife's back. For obvious reasons, she wasn't able to use that message in the pilot!

However, there were enough good messages for Hilary to be able to put together a compilation that could then be turned into a pilot. One of them came through for a lady called Viv Foster. She worked with Hilary and would go on to become a close friend of mine. I gave her a message from a relative, who showed me that she had a chip in her very expensive new fireplace. She was stunned by this because she'd only taken delivery of the fireplace that morning and was terrified that when her husband saw the chip he'd send the fireplace back. It had been such a battle to get the fireplace in the first place that she really didn't want to do that.

I headed back down to Sussex with low expectations. I had had friends in the entertainment industry for years, so I was experienced enough to know that it was probably never going to come to anything. I was wrong, however.

Within a week Hilary rang me up and said we had a

meeting with a company called Living TV, who ran a successful cable channel. They were apparently looking for a British equivalent of John Edward and thought I might fit the bill. They'd watched the pilot and liked it. They now wanted to meet me in person.

I travelled up to the company's offices in Great Portland Street for a meeting with the company's boss, a guy called Richard Woolfe. As I sat down in his office and looked around it was obvious that he'd been involved in *That's Life* with Esther Rantzen. So he had to know what he was doing.

To break the ice, he said: 'So, Colin, have you got any messages for me?'

I jokingly pulled out a card. 'I have a six-month waiting list for private sittings. This is my card and it has my manager's number on it. If you'd like to give him a ring I'm sure we can arrange something,' I said.

He burst out laughing. We got on like a house on fire after that.

We chatted for an hour or so about what sort of series it might be. The format was exactly as Hilary had described it: a mix of theatre-style and one-to-one sittings. We parted company on the basis that they'd be in touch with an offer in the next few days.

By now I admit I was getting a bit more excited about it. I was ecstatic when Hilary called to say they wanted to make twenty episodes initially. It would take around seven days' filming in all and I'd need to make myself available for publicity afterwards. The fee was £20,000 – more than I'd ever earned before.

The initial working title for the series was *The Other Side*. But there was a feeling that this might suggest to people that they should be flipping channels to the other side. So we were asked to come up with another one. I can't remember who came up with it, but the Bruce Willis film *The Sixth Sense* somehow entered the conversation. We had the idea of transposing the capital S of Sixth with the number 6. It looked good and Living TV loved it.

After that, the next job was to 'restyle' my image. I didn't think I looked too bad, but Hilary and the rest of the team thought I should get a younger, slightly trendier haircut. I didn't like it much; it looked like I'd had an old-fashioned pudding bowl haircut. Even worse, I was told I had to keep the same style for the rest of the year for continuity purposes. At least I was allowed to have a little control over my clothes. On stage I always wore a suit and tie and I was adamant that I should do the same on television. That was fine, they said, although there was a strong movement to drop the tie to make it just a little less formal, which I resisted at first.

By February 2002 we were ready to start filming. Doris Stokes' prediction that my career would go into overdrive in my fortieth year came true. We filmed the series in a converted warehouse in the Docklands area of London. We weren't even in a proper television studio. There was this room that they had decked out in white to be my dressing room. My make-up lady was great, very supportive; her name was Shirley Brody. We filmed three episodes a day over a space of seven working days. I kept saying to the production team that I couldn't guarantee it would work. But fortunately things went well. I didn't know whether to put it down to my abilities or whether it was a sign that the spirit world was really pleased that I had been given this platform and they were now working overtime to help me.

All the same, it took us a while to get into our stride. The first audiences consisted of thirty people each. So I was seeing ninety different people a day. And I discovered that working with a television audience was subtly different to working with an audience in a Spiritualist church or a theatre. It wasn't so much the quality; it was the content. There were still these ITC rules which they had to comply with. Although I had no involvement with the audience, there was this whole process behind the scenes, with the production crew and researchers having to vet everybody and get their permission. All the participants had to sign release forms. I had no involvement in those dealings because I'd insisted that I couldn't be caught up in it. So it was very frustrating for me when occasionally I brought through great messages, only for them to end up on the cutting-room floor.

During filming on that first series, one particular message stuck out in this respect. As we filmed one morning, I sensed a very strong male energy. It was a man, probably in his thirties, who had died in the prime of his life. I could feel that he was a physical man – someone who had worked with his hands. I also sensed his name was Joe or Joseph.

When I began to describe this I immediately saw a hand being raised in the audience. It was an attractive young woman. She identified herself as his partner. I'll call her Jennifer. I was now seeing some very graphic and disturbing images. I could see that Joe was in water, where he was trapped between a boat and a jetty. I could feel the boat closing in on him and the panic building inside him as it crushed him. It felt to me like an industrial accident that would have happened in docks, maybe even docks in the area of London where we were filming today.

Jennifer confirmed all this to me. Joe had worked at the nearby docks unloading and loading the vast container ships that sailed up the Thames to London. One day he'd slipped and fallen into the water as a giant cargo ship had been mooring. Before anyone could get to him, he had been crushed to death by the keel of the ship.

Jennifer was in tears when the message ended with Joe telling her he had found peace on the other side and that he wanted her to get on with her life without him. I was really, really pleased with the message. I couldn't believe it a few days later when one of the production team told me that we wouldn't be able to use it in the programme.

'What!' I'd said.

'We can't use it because she wasn't married to him,' they said. 'We need the permission of his next of kin. Jennifer gave us their details but they have refused flat out to let us mention his name or talk about him in any way.'

'But that's ridiculous,' I said.

'I know, but that's the legal situation as far as we are concerned. We can't take the risk of being sued over it,' the production assistant said.

Sadly, as Spiritualist mediums, this is the challenge that faces us when we step out from the confines of our religion (and, after all, I am a Spiritualist) into the world of entertainment. Even today I find the attitude of television's ruling body to be extremely prejudiced towards Spiritualist mediums working in TV. I do not believe they would be allowed to be as prejudiced towards any other religion. The fact that they make TV production companies issue a disclaimer before broadcasts clearly indicates this. I cannot imagine that the Church of England, say, would look kindly on such a disclaimer issued before broadcasts of *Songs of Praise*, for example!

Making a television series was bloody hard work but it was enjoyable. I thought it would be great if the public saw what we mediums actually do. So I really wanted *6ixth Sense* to do much more than simply prove that mediumship and the world of the psychic were legitimate and respectable. I also wanted to touch people's lives and use the ability I had to improve those lives. I knew that I could do this in many ways. I could give comfort and reassurance to people who had lost loved ones but also help those left behind to make positive changes in their own lives. From the beginning I was successful in both.

One of the very first messages that I brought through concerned a little boy whom I connected to his parents. They were in the audience during one of the very first recording sessions when I felt the very strong energy of a child.

His name sounded like Marky or Mikey and he was trying desperately to reach his mother and father. 'His name is Mika,' a lady confirmed, raising her hand in the audience, as people were encouraged to do when they thought a message might be directed at them. It turned out that Mika had died from a very rare genetic disorder. Doctors had tried desperately to save him, but to no avail.

What emerged in the message was that Mika was very proud of the work that his parents had done since his passing. They had set up a charity that was trying to raise money for research into this illness. It was precisely the sort of message that I'd hoped I'd be able to bring out on television: here was an example of a family making a positive out of the massive negative that was the loss of their beautiful child. In the face of their loss, the parents were adamant that their son's memory was going to live on through the work of their charity.

From the very beginning, we always had a wide range of people in the audience and I was always particularly pleased to see people who had doubts or were openly sceptical in the studio, especially when I was able to change their minds in a powerful and transforming way. A Londoner called Harry was a prime example of this and provided some memorable television.

Harry received a very emotional message from his father, like him a tough man from the East End. His father had come through very strongly to me. He wanted to tell Harry that he regretted being so macho and so unwilling to ever admit he was wrong. 'I regret not telling my children that I loved them, because I did,' he told me at one point.

Afterwards Harry admitted on camera that prior to this he had thought the entire idea of mediums and messages from the afterlife was a 'load of codswallop'. When his father came through to him, he admitted it initially had frightened the life out of him. As his father's message revealed itself he moved from fear to revelation.

When his dad had told him about his regrets, he'd had his eyes opened to his own failings. He and his family came back for a second time to another filming session at which they told me the experience had changed Harry completely. 'One minute I was wondering why I was here listening to what I thought was a load of old rubbish and the next I heard that message. It really was something. The question of whether Dad loved us or not when we were kids really tormented me, because I just never knew if he did,' Harry told me.

His family were grateful as well. 'He has definitely changed for the better in many ways, one of them being that he will now discuss his feelings with us and won't shy away from them like he did before,' Harry's daughter Hayley told me. 'You made my dad very happy. It also made him quite sad because I think he wished he'd known earlier. Since the reading he's been more open and a lot happier. He even cuddles my brother!'

In a similar vein, I received a message from the grandfather of a man called Johnny. He, again, was something of a tough nut. His grandfather showed me some disturbing images of a dart being fired. Johnny admitted that he and his mates used to play a game of chicken where they fired darts, William Tell-style, at people with apples on their heads.

He also admitted performing mock 'crucifixions' in the graveyard of a local church with some mates. As his grandfather's message continued, however, I got the very strong feeling that it was mostly concerned with the fact that Johnny had behaved in this same, brutish way to his brother, Peter.

At one point I was shown an image of someone

pushing Peter's head down a toilet. Again, Johnny admitted to it, laughing almost as if he was proud of it. He then confessed that he had always been a bit 'tough' on Peter, his older and more studious brother. They were estranged at the time.

Slowly but surely, Johnny's 'Jack the Lad' demeanour became more and more serious as the message continued. His grandfather had clearly wanted to get a particular message through – and eventually the penny dropped. 'I must admit I've neglected him a bit recently,' Johnny said as his grandfather put more thoughts into my head about Peter. 'He rings me up quite a bit but I don't bother ringing him back. I just feel I have nothing in common with him. But I must ring him, that's what my granddad's saying.'

By the end of the message, Johnny looked thoroughly ashamed of himself. As he left the studio that afternoon, I got the very strong sense that he was going to make amends with his brother very soon.

As well as sceptics, we also saw a lot of people who had lost their faith. One was a lady called Elaine, who received a message from her brother, Bernard. He had died at the age of only thirty-three in a mysterious road accident a couple of Christmases earlier. His large Irish family, especially Elaine and her mother, had been totally devastated, so much so that they had given up going to church.

Elaine told me that her mother couldn't understand how God had done this to her, a common feeling among the bereaved. Bernard told Elaine that he wanted his mother to return to the Church. He wanted some other changes too. The family had started making a biannual pilgrimage to the spot where it had happened. In his message, Bernard asked them to stop doing that because it was making things worse rather than better for his mother.

Last but not least, he also wanted Elaine to 'let go' of her grief over his passing.

Elaine blamed herself for his death. Elaine had nine brothers in all but was closest to Bernard, who was a similar age to her. He had been living with her in London and was heading back to her house from the family home in Ireland when the accident happened. Her partner, John, was sitting next to her in the studio and told me very movingly of the pain she'd been going through.

As Elaine agreed to listen to her brother's plea for her to let him go, John said on camera, 'For me personally, there is relief in the thought that Elaine will maybe let go now and find her faith again. Because before she couldn't and there would be tears to the point where it's very hard to take, just watching her in pain.' There were a few tears shed in the audience too as he said those words.

When Bernard's energy had faded and his message come to an end, I felt a very powerful sense of having helped not one but several people. Again, I was less concerned with making good television than I was with making people's lives better or at least more bearable than they had been before they came into the studio.

I turned forty in May 2002 but didn't celebrate my birthday. There was still too much to do. *6ixth Sense* was going to be premiered on Living TV's new Paranormal Zone in May 2002. The two programmes they were promoting most were *6ixth Sense* with me and *Most Haunted* with Derek Acorah and Yvette Fielding, so I had to do press interviews. We also went to the Sky TV centre in Livingston, Scotland so that they knew what they were selling.

Sky magazine did an interview with me and Derek. That was the point when I became friends with Derek and his wife Gwen. Derek had some experience of television and knew the impact it could have on your career. I was still naive about this at the time and kept talking about how I was still intending to focus on my private sittings. I still thought 'this has been fun' but it's not going to last. Working in The Spirit Lodge was still going to be my 'bread and butter'.

One day, as we were travelling to an interview together, and I was fretting about having missed a call about a sitting I was supposed to be doing the following day, Gwen started laughing.

'What is it?' I said.

'Trust me, darling, when this goes on television you won't have time to worry about any of that.'

15 | Highs and Lows

ONE day in May 2002 my life changed forever.

It began as an ordinary day. It was rubbish collection day so when I got up I went downstairs to put the bin out. The dustcart happened to be passing down the street at that moment and one of the regular binmen stopped and shouted at me, 'Morning, Colin – hear you're on television today.'

'How did you know that?' I said.

'Your mum told us.'

She'd been round the entire neighbourhood, apparently.

The first episode went out at 1 pm and was repeated again at 6 pm. Hilary called me to say that the audience figures had been very good but we obviously needed to see some more ratings data. I was still of the view that this had been a fun experiment, and carried on organising my normal life.

We were two weeks into the series being broadcast when Hilary rang me up. She sounded very excited. 'I've just had a phone call from Richard Woolfe. Whatever you've got planned for the rest of the year, cancel it. We've been commissioned to do another forty shows – and we've got to start soon,' she said.

They were obviously pleased with it. So in July we were back in the studio again, this time in the London Studios on the South Bank. It was a proper television studio with a proper dressing room. I'd arrived!

The impact on my life was incredible. Suddenly I was on television every day of the week, every day of the year, in countries across the world. My phone was ringing nonstop with offers for me to make appearances at events and seminars in places I'd never even heard of. Whenever I switched on my email, the number of requests for sittings had increased by a few thousand.

A few weeks after the second series was commissioned I saw Derek Acorah's wife, Gwen, at a gathering and she came up to me, laughing. 'See, I told you, didn't I?' she said.

For once I found myself unable to say anything.

All the same, I was determined to continue with my other work for as long as I could. A part of me was still convinced that television would be a flash in the pan and I didn't want to turn my back on the community that had supported me to this point. Running as many classes and seances as I'd done previously was a challenge, however. As for sittings, it was now impossible for me to cope with the demand, so I had to introduce a strict booking policy. Soon there was a waiting list of between three and six years. This, of course, didn't go down well with some people.

One evening I got a phone call at home. I picked up to hear a very loud, American voice barking down the line. 'Hi, I'm calling you from Los Angeles and my name is So-and-so,' he said. 'I guess you've heard of me?'

I hadn't. I had no idea who he was but said nothing.

'Listen, I'm gonna send you flight tickets. I want you on a plane on Saturday, I'm gonna to fly you to Los Angeles. We're organising this seance. Some of the biggest names in Hollywood are gonna be there,' he went on, before reeling off what was, I had to admit, a pretty impressive list of names – including famous actors, actresses and politicians who were very familiar to me. 'It's gonna be great, everything will be looked after and we are gonna pay you a bucketful of money, on the subject of which—' he went on.

It was at that point that I cut him off. 'I'm sorry but I'm not available,' I said.

There was a brief silence. Then: 'What do you mean, you're not available?'

'Exactly what I say. I'm booked up to do other things. I have a seminar this weekend and I have clients booked who have been on my waiting list for three months. I can't just drop everything to come to Los Angeles. I can't let them down,' I said.

'Didn't you hear who I said was gonna be there?' the man said, clearly irritated now.

'Yes, I did, but you didn't hear what I just said. I'm not available and I can't be bought, not by you or anyone else,' I said before promptly putting down the phone.

I may not have flown out to Hollywood to sit for some of the world's biggest movie stars, but at home, I was beginning to get some very well-known clients. I'd had one or two in the past, but as my fame spread I found myself being approached by a whole raft of celebrities, politicians and members of royal families.

I've never approved of the fact that some mediums are very indiscreet about who they have sat for. Seeing a medium is like a consultation with a doctor. It should be private and confidential. Now, if that famous person wants to make it public knowledge that they have a relationship with a medium then that is fine. The pop star, Suzi Quatro, for instance, has been publicly supportive of my work, while *Only Fools And Horses* actor Nicholas Lyndhurst and his wife became personal friends after they attended a few of my public performances.

But otherwise I keep my own counsel. Suffice it to say, however, that in the years that followed, I sat for some extremely prominent people, from all walks of life, including show business, politics, business – even religion. I also had several clients who were members of some of Europe's most notable royal houses. I have never divulged their names, nor will I now. And I would always go to great lengths to protect their privacy when they visited me – although it didn't always work.

One day, around this time, I got a phone call from a member of staff at the London residence of a prominent European royal family, asking if the head of the family could visit me for a sitting. I agreed and made sure the house was empty for his visit. The very distinguished man arrived in a large, smart limousine, and was quickly spirited into the house from where we made our way down to the Lodge.

We then spent the best part of an hour together. The reading went extremely well. I was able to make contact with his father, with whom he'd had a difficult relationship. After it was over, I invited him back into the house for a coffee, to which he agreed.

Unfortunately, my mother used to have this terrible habit of turning up unannounced. She also had a particular knack of turning up at the wrong moment. Today, as I escorted my royal guest into the house, she was standing in the kitchen. For a moment I wondered whether she'd recognise him. I'd seen him on television many times. But fortunately she didn't.

I couldn't breach his confidentiality by saying who he was, so – typically – my mother began asking questions. 'So, darling, you're not from this country, are you?' she said.

I was so embarrassed I wanted the ground to open up and swallow me.

'No, my family has a very strong connection to X,' he said.

'Oh, that's a lovely country. Have you ever been to

X? My husband and I went there once and we had an amazing time. We just spent all day on the beach and all the evenings in the restaurants,' she said, describing a beautiful resort they had been to a couple of summers earlier.

'Ah yes, I know it,' he said. 'My family has a summer residence there.'

That was enough to set my mum off even more. The weak and sickly lady of a few years earlier had disappeared and she was back to her old self.

To my amazement he was happy to chat for a little longer. But when he finished his coffee he asked me to check if his chauffeur was outside. I ran to the front and took a look. The car was sitting there waiting, as arranged.

'In that case, Mr Fry, I will say thank you again and bid you farewell. Lovely to meet you too, Mrs Fry,' he said, extending his hand.

'Ah, what a lovely gentleman!' my mother said a few moments later as we watched the car gliding away. 'Who was he?'

I just looked at her and smiled. 'That was the King of X,' I said.

She almost dropped her coffee cup. 'Why the hell didn't you tell me, I'd have curtsied,' she said.

The King was far from the last member of royalty to visit me. Some of my clients came from show business royalty, however.

Not long after his royal visit, I had one from another rather grand individual, this time an American lady. It turned out she had made the booking under a false name, as a Miss Gibson. When she turned up it was all a bit Gloria Swanson. She had a headscarf on and dark glasses. Her minder led her into the house and then down into the Lodge, checking that her path was clear – as if she was the First Lady or something.

The two of us sat down in the privacy of the Lodge and I began taking her through the regular formalities that I always went through. I explained that I could make no promises: that we might get a message, but equally we might not.

'I understand,' she said.

'Shall we make a start then?' I said.

'Yes, please go ahead,' she nodded.

As she did so I felt a familiar feeling. 'No, don't do this to me,' I said to myself. I could feel the strange sleepiness I encounter when I go into a trance in a seance. The spirit world was taking me away with them. The last thing I remember seeing was the lady's face.

When I came around, I looked at the clock. I had been gone for almost an hour. The lady was still there, looking very relaxed and happy and pleased to see me restored to my normal state.

'I'm so sorry,' I said. 'That hasn't happened to me before during a reading.'

She was all smiles and told me not to worry. 'It doesn't matter, I've had the most wonderful conversation with my mother,' she said. It was at this point that she revealed her identity. She was the daughter of one of the most famous actresses in the history of Hollywood, and – I should add – a personal favourite of mine.

This actress had come through to me and others in seances that I'd attended over the years. In particular, she'd come through at a seance I'd conducted at The Spirit Lodge only six months earlier, when she'd been quite emotional and a little angry. The lady's later life was very troubled and she'd fought a long and well documented battle against alcoholism and addiction. This daughter and her older sister were both very young when she died. The older sister had gone on to be a very famous entertainer herself, but was suffering from the same problems that had afflicted her mother's career.

'I had heard that my mother had been coming through in your seances, but I needed to come incognito to know if it was true,' the lady said as we chatted over a cup of tea. 'She told me that my sister has to change, and change soon, otherwise it is going to end the same way for her as it did for my mother.'

It was obvious that the communication had been hugely important for this lady. 'I never felt like I knew my mother,' she explained. 'That's why I've tried a few times to make a connection with her through a medium. I have tried in America but never really had much success. What you did today was remarkable and I can't thank you enough for it. It felt like I was talking to my mother properly for the first time in my life.'

As she gathered her things together and prepared to leave, I couldn't resist mentioning the recent occasion when I'd refused an invitation to go over and sit for a collection of movie stars at short notice.

'Good for you,' she said, when I explained what I'd said to the pushy producer. 'It's nice to hear that someone can still say no.'

'No' was a word I was learning to say to other people too . . . Professionally, my career had skyrocketed. Although I have never accepted the mantle of celebrity very well, I had become one. I would go into a department store and get discounts because of who I was. I would be able to get tables at well-known restaurants simply by mentioning my name. It wasn't an unpleasant thing. In fact, it could be quite funny, like the occasion I went to Selfridges in London to do some shopping.

It had been decided that I needed a new wardrobe for a new series of the TV show. The producers wanted me to have a slightly slicker, more businesslike sort of image.

So my management had booked a personal shopper for me at the store. When my TV dresser and I got to the area where you are supposed to meet your personal shopper, we were greeted by this very smartly dressed little Japanese chap. He was typically polite. He gave a little bow and said: 'Mr Fry, it is so nice to see you.'

I had a pretty good idea what I wanted to buy, so I asked him to lead me to the suits section and we set off together. I needed to get a selection of suits, shirts, belts and some nice ties. So I began rummaging through the racks of smart clothes, grabbing a few items to try on and then heading into the changing room. Each time I did so the personal shopper would carry the clothes for me and each time I chose something I liked, he would smile and say: 'Oh, Mr Fry, it looks so good on you, it really suits you.'

All in all we probably spent more than an hour wandering around the menswear department and by the end you could hardly see the personal shopper for clothes. He wasn't very tall and was buried underneath a mountain of jackets and shirts and accessories. We then returned to the personal shopper area where there was a till.

When we got there a lady came forward, looking a bit baffled. 'Mr Fry, we were expecting you about an hour and a half ago,' she said. 'We'd been told that you wanted to use our personal shopper service.'

I looked as confused as her, I'm sure. I turned and pointed towards the Japanese guy. When I explained that he'd shown me around, the lady just shook her head and said: 'I have no idea who he is.'

It didn't remain a mystery for too long. Sensing what was going on, my 'personal shopper' laid all the clothes on the counter, reached into his coat pocket and fished out a small notebook and pen, which he then handed to me. 'Mr Fry, could I ask you for your autograph now?'

I burst into hysterical laughter. He didn't even work there.

On the face of it, being recognised and being regarded as 'famous', whatever that may mean, is very glamorous. People aspire to become celebrities for that reason. But, of course, we all know that it's not that simple and, unfortunately, there was a downside to my new-found fame. My success was causing huge conflict at home. My relationship with Chris had deteriorated to the point where we were barely speaking.

The break-up of a relationship is always complicated; there are always many root causes. And so it was with us. There were a few reasons why we'd drifted apart, one of which was that I was living a life that Chris wanted no part of. Chris was a highly intelligent guy, he had a MENSA gold certificate. And because of that he approached life in a way that was very logical. He couldn't understand how I lived on my emotions in the way that I did. I had always made decisions based on what I felt, not on what was logical, and that had led to conflict between us.

I remember asking him, 'Do you love me?' and his

reply to me: 'In my own way' – but that was never enough for me. I used to ask him: 'Do you believe in what I do?' His answer was always the same: 'No, but I believe in you, Colin, and if you believe in what you are doing, then so do I.'

This was having an inevitable impact on my professional life because, at that point in my career, Chris was technically supposed to be managing me, while my friend Vince was supposed to be my PA. However, as things began to deteriorate Vince was very conflicted about the problems that Chris and I were having, because he was a friend to us both. He felt, quite understandably, that he was caught in the middle.

Our relationship was going to the dogs and there were particular aspects of Chris's behaviour that I found very hard to live with, but which I'd rather not go into detail about here. It's enough to say that, for a period of about a year before we split up, I was working nonstop, and would come back home from a tour date or a TV recording to find Chris fast asleep on the sofa, an empty glass at his side. So I would take myself off to the Lodge at the bottom of the garden, where I would sleep on a camp bed.

Inevitably, the state of my relationship with Chris affected me. For a while I found that I was turning to drink and drugs in a misguided attempt to keep myself sane. For about twelve months I tried to blot it all out, smoking weed or occasionally snorting cocaine, something I'd always been so adamantly against. It was a measure of how low I was. Of course, I was now occupying a world where it wasn't hard to get hold of drugs. I had begun to realise that there is a dark side to the world of entertainment.

I was being invited to parties and functions and being told by people, 'Oh, you look tired, do you need something to help you?' So I got sucked into it. I am not afraid to admit it was a shameful – but thankfully brief – period of my life. It went on for about a year, but I was able to see the damage it was doing to me and stopped. If I hadn't been the age I was and if I hadn't had the life experiences I'd had, then it could have been the end of me. It was a brief and shameful time, but luckily I got out of it as quickly as I got into it.

It was ironic: I was on a professional high, but on a personal level I was at one of the lowest points in my life. After twenty-two years, I could not put any more effort into my relationship. It wasn't working and I recognised that it hadn't been working for a very long time.

One night I got back from a demonstration and found Chris lying asleep on the sofa once more. I just looked at him once and – to my eternal shame – thought to myself, 'Why don't you just die?' I went to bed and locked the door and made the decision that night: 'Tomorrow this had to end.' It was 2003.

Ending a relationship is never easy. There is always pain. Chris and I came to an arrangement and he moved out of the home. As a friend of us both, Vince found it very difficult and so I parted company with him as well. I'm pleased to say that these days I'm on friendly terms with both Chris and Vince, but it was a difficult time back then. Fortunately, I had a lot of other friends – as well as a lot of wisdom gained from those I encountered in my work – that I could draw upon. In particular, I remembered something that Ida had taught me, that people serve a purpose in your life. It's painful when you have to part from them, but ultimately it is for the best.

It's one of the hard lessons you have to learn in life and I learned it then. What made it easier, however, was another piece of wisdom I'd learned: that when one door closes, inevitably another one opens. And so it proved for me.

It seems to be a recurring theme in my life that whenever I've wanted or needed somebody to share with or help me, the right person will always come along sooner or later. It was in the wake of my break-up with Chris that I met someone who was to become one of my closest friends.

I met Eden James at a party in Brighton. We'd hit it off immediately, I think because we'd sensed we were kindred spirits going through similar difficulties. We were both at incredibly low points in our lives at the time, having been through the end of relationships. Ours was never an intimate relationship; we just sensed that each of us was at an emotional low and were able to give each other the support we needed. Quite soon after meeting him I asked him to become my driver and soon after that my manager.

I really like the fact that when we met he didn't have a clue what I did for a living.

I just told him that I worked in the 'entertainment industry'. It was only when we were walking through Churchill Square in Brighton one day and a lady ran up to me asking for an autograph that he realised I was some kind of celebrity. For that reason he grounded me; he gave me an escape from all the bullshit of celebrity, which was something I badly needed at that time.

I regarded myself as a well-known medium, not a celebrity. I really didn't like that label very much at all. I was working with a lot of people who were used to working in the world of entertainment and boosting the popularity and ego of the person they were representing. But they weren't interested in – and didn't really understand – what it was that I did. I frequently had to explain to people that I wasn't some kind of fortune teller and that I didn't summon the dead.

I tried to be very patient but there were times when it could be frustrating. During the World Cup in 2006, one of the PR people from the programme had come to me and told me about this 'great opportunity' that they'd set up for me. 'You are going to go and appear on the World Cup video with Ant and Dec and try to heal David Beckham's foot,' she said.

It's not often I swear at people, especially young women, but I couldn't stop myself. 'You must be f***ing joking,' I said.

'Why?' she said. 'It's a great opportunity for you.'

'It's undignified and it's actually making a mockery of what I do,' I said, before storming out of the room. Some people just didn't get what I did – and what I didn't do.

There was a real conflict over my refusal because arrangements had been made, and the producer of the show, Richard Woolfe, came and found me in my dressing room to talk it through.

I had a wonderful time working with Living TV but there were times where I felt like I was back in the school situation. Once again I felt as though I was a square peg that people were trying to squeeze into a round hole – and now I wasn't going to put up with it any longer. I'd promised myself that wouldn't happen again.

16 | Stage Presence

ONE Monday evening in 2005 I arrived at the famous Playhouse in Edinburgh, one of Scotland's oldest and most famous theatres, as part of a huge national tour organised by the TV production company, IPM. It was a vast auditorium capable of holding 3,000 people. To my surprise, when I got to my dressing room there was a beautiful bunch of flowers and a very large bottle of champagne sitting on my dressing table. There was also a note from the owners, saying: 'Congratulations, Colin Fry! You are the first person in twenty-two years to sell out the Playhouse on a Monday night.'

It wasn't such an uncommon occurrence for me. Months earlier, when I had been in New Zealand, where I was very popular, the promoter had told me that mine was the biggest sell-out tour he'd had in New Zealand since Tina Turner had been there. It was so crazy that I had to have a professional bodyguard as I travelled around cities like Hamilton, Wellington and Auckland. I had to accept that in the public forum I would be mobbed.

Such was the power of television and such was the phenomenal success of *6ixth Sense*. Between 2002 and 2005 we had made one hundred and forty episodes of the series. The show had been sold to countless overseas territories where, as in the UK, it was broadcast two or even three times a day. Hilary used to joke that at any time of the day or night, somewhere in the world, someone was watching Colin Fry. 'Now there aren't many people who can say that,' she used to smile.

With the series over and new television projects in the pipeline, IPM had decided to start organising a series of live appearances. The show would remain pretty much the same for the next four years. I'd demonstrate for around two hours, often supported by a second medium, and concentrating totally on delivering as many meaningful messages as I could to the assembled audience. I was conducting an annual solo tour as well as a joint tour, *The Best of British Mediumship* with Tony Stockwell, the highlight being when we appeared at the London Palladium, which was filmed for TV and later released as a DVD. The DVD featured a one-to-one reading with Katherine Jenkins, which she kindly mentioned in her autobiography.

Perhaps it was the little drama-loving boy in me that adored the experience of being on a stage with the audience watching me. Perhaps it was the knowledge that the spirit world kept telling me how much they liked what I was doing. Whatever the explanation, I absolutely loved performing live at that point in my life. More than anything I valued the connection I felt with a worldwide audience that had seen me demonstrate on television. Once again I was reminded of Doris Stokes' prediction all those years earlier. I had spread the word about Spiritualism and mediumship to the four corners of the globe. It made me rather proud, I have to say.

I never lost sight of my responsibility. I always tried to remember the words of another huge influence: Leslie Flint. His belief was that mediums are here on earth to do good. I tried to do that every time I stepped on stage, no matter where it was. I like to think I've succeeded.

My live shows were very much like the television series in the sense that I never knew what was going to come my way once I'd finished my introductory speech and the house lights went on to reveal the audience. 'Expect the unexpected' became my motto.

During those years touring the UK and beyond, I passed on hundreds of messages. Because I am the 'vessel', the messenger who is helping spirits to communicate, the content of the majority of these messages is almost always forgotten by me. It is only through watching videos of the stage performances or television shows that I can remember some of them ever happened. But there are others that I will never forget. My life has always been a journey of discovery.

These messages stick in the memory because of the impact they had not just on the recipients but on me as well. They taught me so much. I will share with you two of them, delivered by very different people to very different families, but both remarkable testaments to the universal healing power of love.

One of the most emotional messages I gave during that period of my life as a performing medium happened at a theatre in Rhyl in North Wales. It came from the spirit of a very young child.

The child had come through very strongly to me and was identified by his mother and father immediately when he said, 'Tell Mum that I passed at five past two.'

I feel emotional whenever I am in the presence of a child that has passed at a very young age. I know the pain and suffering this has caused and find it hard sometimes to deal with the rawness of those emotions. In this case, the baby's parents were very composed and brave, which helped me keep it together.

At one point the baby showed me an image of a room filled with blue balloons. He also showed me some bread being shoved into a video recorder. The father smiled at this memory for some reason. The baby also showed me an older boy, his brother. It was an aerial image as if he was hovering over him while he was playing football.

People come to me, broadly speaking, for two

reasons: to get the answer to a specific question or issue surrounding the passing of a loved one, or simply to be reassured that the loved one has passed over safely and is happy and being cared for in the afterlife.

It was clear to me that this couple were here for the second reason. They wanted to know that their baby was safe. I was able to reassure them that he was. As the message continued I felt the presence of a second person, an older woman.

'She's holding his hand,' I said. I also got the strong sense that she was there when the baby had passed over and had died more recently. The date, 17 March, came through very strongly. The lady cried at this and said it was her mother's birthday. She then confirmed that her mother was in spirit.

'She is looking after your baby and says he is safe and well,' I said. It is very difficult to convey meaningful and resonant messages from such a new baby because they have no memories to communicate through. I got the overwhelming sense that this baby had passed over very, very young. But the baby did show me an image of them taking photographs. He then gave me a sentence that seemed again to connect very strongly with the couple: 'He wants you to think of him as he was in the photographs, not as he was when the doctors had intervened,' I said.

I spoke to the couple afterwards and they explained to me the full meaning of the message. The mother's name was Kelly. Towards the end of her second pregnancy doctors had detected a problem with the child. It had a severe and very rare genetic disorder. It wasn't an option for them to terminate the pregnancy, not least because it could have endangered Kelly's life. So the decision was made that she would give birth to the baby, knowing that he would only live for a few hours. Kelly and her husband, Dean, did all they could to make those few hours as memorable as possible, decorating the room with blue balloons and taking photographs. Their other son was also there to meet and then say goodbye to his baby brother.

They told me that the image of the bread being shoved in the video player showed something that the little boy had done quite recently. They told me he was also a very keen footballer and was always out and about kicking a ball around. They were incredibly touched by the thought that their baby was somehow watching down on his older brother from above.

It must have been the most heart-rending situation to go through. I can't imagine what it must be like to witness the miracle of birth knowing that it will be followed by the tragedy of death within the space of a few short hours. It made the message I had been able to deliver to them all the more powerful and important.

What was particularly gratifying for me as I toured the UK and beyond, was the diversity of people who were coming to see me, having watched me on television. There was a time when mediums performed to theatres made up of 99 per cent women, and middle-aged or elderly women at that. Thanks to the success of *6ixth Sense* that demographic had changed completely. Every night I looked out into the audience and saw people of all ages: sons, daughters, mothers, fathers, aunts, grandfathers and grandmothers. Often they came along as a group.

I felt like the goal that I had set myself when I'd agreed to do television had somehow been met. I'd spread the word about mediumship to a new generation. It was especially pleasing because the younger generation suffer from the loss of loved ones every bit as much as their older relatives. Often they suffer more.

That was the case with another remarkable message that I brought through around this time when I was on stage in the north of England. I felt myself in the presence of a boy who wanted to connect with his family – and his brother in particular.

Four members of his family were there in the audience: his mother, his two sisters and a brother. But the brother he needed to contact was not there, for some reason. This seemed to make the boy agitated and angry. He needed to ask the brother to give someone his forgiveness.

Most messages I received were relatively benign. A large proportion of them came from people who simply wanted to make contact. There was something

a lot more desperate about this particular communication, however. It was as if an entire family's life
depended on it.

I learned a little during the message itself. The
spirit talked to his mother, reassuring her that he was
safe on the other side. He sent his love to all the
family, emphasising the world 'all' for some reason I
didn't understand at the time. The brother who was in
the theatre sat in his seat crying uncontrollably
throughout. When the message faded, I felt I'd not
done it justice and asked that he come to talk to me
after the show had finished. Wiping the tears from his
eyes, he agreed.

By now I had got used to the fact that people
would wait to speak to me after the show had ended.
Many of them hadn't received a message and were still
hoping for something. Others simply wanted to say
thank you for the message they had received. Some
wanted a deeper explanation. So it took me a while to
get to the brother after the curtain came down. I could
see him standing patiently in the foyer.

'I'm so sorry to keep you waiting, mate,' I said
when I finally got to him.

Almost immediately, I felt the presence of his
brother again. This was unusual and only underlined
my feeling that there was a really important message
that simply had to be allowed to come through. In a
remarkable sequence of images and words, the older
brother began to show me the story of his family.

I saw that this lad was the younger brother of the spirit who had come through to me. They had been through a terrible childhood together. Their father had abandoned them when they were small, leaving the older brother to take on the role of breadwinner in the family. He had been bright and hopeful of going to college. But those dreams had been dashed by the need to put food on the table for his mother and siblings.

The younger brother nodded throughout this, simply saying, 'That's right, that's right.' He nodded vigorously when I told him that I had the feeling he had been a real wild child and had been hyperactive and constantly in trouble. 'Yes, that's true,' he said.

I saw that he had fallen into drug abuse, developed a heroin habit and from there turned to crime to support his addiction. It was a sad and very familiar story, one that was far too common at the time, and still is, of course.

His spirit brother then showed me that things got so bad that his mother kicked his younger brother out of the house. It sent him into even more of a downward spiral. He'd broken back into his family's home and stolen all their possessions, including the television. His older brother had snapped at this point and confronted him. He had done so at the worst possible moment.

The younger brother remained rigid, staring at the floor as I described what I was now being shown by his brother in spirit. His brother had knocked on the door of the place where he lived, shouting that he should come outside. The younger brother had been in a hyper-anxious state because he was waiting for his supplier to deliver him his next fix of heroin. The two brothers exchanged words. The younger one was angry about being told what to do. Somehow a knife appeared. I was suddenly being shown an image of a flashing blade, blood and the older brother lying on the floor.

As I described this the young man was in floods of tears once more. But he pulled himself together to confirm what I'd described was true. 'I was off my head, I had no idea what I was doing,' he told me. 'Before I knew it I'd killed my own brother.'

He told me that he had been given a jail sentence, but that it had been reduced because he had rehabilitated himself and kicked his heroin habit. But he had been released from prison only weeks earlier and it had been his mother's idea that he come along tonight.

It was then that his brother was finally able to get across the message that he had been so desperate to transmit. He showed me the third brother, the one who wasn't with his family that night and who, I learned, had been utterly unable to forgive this young man for what he had done. The message from the afterlife was that the third brother had to forgive; he had to accept his surviving brother back into the family, or it would kill them too.

The young man in spirit demonstrated his own forgiveness as well. 'He is telling me that if you do something good with your life he will be behind you every step of the way,' I said.

Forgiveness is one of the most important and enduring principles in religions everywhere. And, after three decades working as a medium, I know it is one of the most powerful principles in the afterlife too. The two brothers illustrated the power of that simple idea more eloquently than any other message I had received then, and it remains that way today. They taught me a lesson I will never, ever forget.

One day in the summer of 2005 I went to a friend's party in Brighton. It was a lovely, bright sunny day and the party was great fun, full of familiar faces but some new and interesting ones as well. Among those I got talking to was a young guy called Mikey. He was a nice, good-looking guy with a fresh, 'no bullshit' attitude to life. What made him even more attractive was the fact that he had absolutely no idea who I was. With all the nonsense that was now surrounding me, it was a real breath of fresh air to be judged purely as myself rather than 'Colin Fry the TV personality'.

Two years had passed since I'd broken up with Chris, but I was still badly bruised. I hadn't had a relationship since and I had no real thought of forming a serious, long-term relationship now. But there was something that drew me to this guy immediately. We agreed to meet up again and started seeing each other for a drink or a meal in Brighton.

At that time I was working hard on tour, appearing in shows like *The Best of British Mediumship* with Tony Stockwell and *Colin Fry Live*. But I also had a long trip to make to New Zealand, where I'd agreed to appear in a tour called *The Happy Medium* and do some television work. So I didn't see much of Mikey until the beginning of the autumn.

At that point I was already planning a Christmas and New Year break over in Ramsberg with friends. Having a drink with Mikey one night in Haywards Heath I suggested that he come over. 'It will be fun, it's a great place,' I told him.

Mikey told me that the situation was a bit complicated. He was caring for a guy called John, who had been his foster father. John was ill and needed someone to keep an eye on him.

Ramsberg is such a wonderful, spiritual place. It's an ideal place for people to get over illness. I thought it made total sense for him to bring John along as well, so invited them both. It was agreed.

By now I had taken a huge decision and committed myself to buying the Swedish centre. The family had found themselves in financial difficulties and I had decided to help them out. I had never been someone for whom money was important. I was fortunate to have some now because of the success of my television series. Keeping the centre going was important to me – so I did what I felt was right. There were already big plans for a new roof, a complete redecoration of the interior and all sorts of things. The place was already draining money from my accounts.

Some friends had warned me against investing, predicting it would turn into a 'money pit' that would eat up every penny I had. But I didn't care. I'd invested my money wisely, mainly by acquiring a much bigger home in a small village in the Sussex countryside. The Spirit Lodge remained at the bottom of the garden in my old house where, as far as I was aware, it had been converted back into a normal garden shed or perhaps a summerhouse.

I decided that I would no longer have a centre at my house. Home had to be an escape and a retreat from my increasingly hectic professional life.

I'd already come up with ways for the centre in Sweden to generate its own income. As well as running classes and lecturing, I also ran the college as a holiday retreat. The previous Christmas I had advertised it as the perfect location for people who had no family, or who wanted to be on their own for Christmas, or who just wanted to experience an alternative holiday season. I'd planned on doing the same thing again this year.

And so it was that, in December 2005, Mikey, John, Eden and I headed to Sweden for Christmas and New Year. I warned Mikey that I was going to be very tied up over there. But I was true to my word and once more spent Christmas Day in the kitchen, up to my ears in turkey, roast potatoes and sprouts. By then, however, it was clear that there was something else going on between us. Not to put too fine a point on it, Mikey and I were falling in love.

I had always been someone who made decisions based on emotions rather than logic. When I got back to England, I followed my heart and asked Mikey to move into my new house. He did so at the end of January.

There were plenty of people who predicted the relationship wouldn't last. Some based it on our age gap, others on the fact that we hadn't known each other very long. My father still found it a problem to deal with my sexuality, even after twenty years. He also had difficulty accepting Mikey. But to be honest I didn't care. I knew that this time I was with someone who loved me. It didn't feel like it had done with Chris. Mikey didn't love me 'in his own way', but in a very real way. I probably felt loved for the first time in my life in that respect. I couldn't remember ever being so happy.

By the autumn of that year we'd decided to get married. Civil partnerships had only become law in the UK about a year earlier. We looked into having a ceremony at Haywards Heath Register Office and booked it for 22 December, the first anniversary of our getting together in Sweden.

It was a wonderful day. However, despite everything we'd been through and the new understanding I thought we had, my dad didn't come. I felt offended by this but refused to let it spoil my and Mikey's happiness. My brother was also absent but my mother and niece were there, as were about forty friends, including some from show business like Nicholas Lyndhurst and his wife. Hilary Goodman and her husband Craig came along, as did my fellow medium Tony Stockwell. The service itself was lovely. The registrar went to a lot of extra effort to make it a special day. We then headed back to a local community hall where we had a champagne reception and ate an amazing chocolate cake.

We ended the day by inviting about twenty people back to the house until 10 pm, at which point we kicked everyone out. It marked the beginning of a new phase in my life and career. Yet another door had opened, and another one was about to close.

17 | Leap of Faith

IN 2009, to the sound of thunderous applause from the 2,500 or so people in the sell-out audience, I walked out onto the stage of the Hammersmith Apollo in London. Standing alongside me were Derek Acorah and a third medium, TJ Higgs. Together we were performing as 'The Three Mediums'.

As I looked out from the stage, I could see a host of familiar faces in the audience below. Friends were sitting in the front rows, all beaming with pride. Eden and many other close friends were also there. It was, in many ways, the highlight of my professional career, the ultimate achievement in all the years I'd been demonstrating. There I was standing on the stage of the Hammersmith Apollo, probably the most famous and prestigious theatre in London and maybe the world. If someone had told me that would be my destiny when I was growing up, I would have laughed at them. It was a long way from the career as a dustman that the secondary school teacher had predicted for me.

And yet, as I soaked up the applause, somewhere

at the back of my mind there was a tiny voice telling me that I should savour this moment. Change was in the wind once more. I was once again approaching a crossroads in my life.

I had been working with the TV production company IPM for seven years by now. Since the phenomenal success of *6ixth Sense*, we'd worked on a series of projects together, from television series to stage tours like *The Three Mediums*, which I had done previously with Derek Acorah and Tony Stockwell, as well as *The Best of British Mediumship* and *Colin Fry Live*. As I've already mentioned, I had continued to travel the world, making *The Happy Medium* series in New Zealand and demonstrating in Ireland and Scandinavia. In particular, I'd built myself an even bigger global reputation thanks to a television series called *Psychic Private Eyes*.

It had been Hilary who had come up with the idea for the show, which had been created for a television station called Zone Reality, now CBS Reality. The programme featured me and two other mediums, TJ Higgs and Tony Stockwell, investigating unsolved crimes using our psychic and mediumistic abilities. Its success was quite ironic really because initially I didn't want to do it. I'd done work to help the police in the past, but had always kept it private.

I'd become involved in a case when I first began working professionally as a medium. A senior chief inspector, whose wife had come to The Spirit Lodge on a regular basis for sittings, asked me whether I'd be willing to take a look at a particularly grisly and sinister case.

A day or two later I'd been taken to a remote Sussex forest in the dead of night. I'd been taken to the spot where a passerby had found a male body, with its head, feet and hands removed. The body had been transferred to the mortuary by the time I got there but there had still been traces of blood and other signs of activity that I had been able to work with psychically.

I had picked up on a number of images, including a house on a High Street and numbers: 33 and 37. I also saw a package lying at the bottom of what looked like a well. With the police, I'd gone along to the nearest village where, using the information I'd given them, we found ourselves in a garden. At the bottom of a well, officers had found a package of pornographic videos.

My involvement was peripheral. But I was told that the case involved a gang that was trading in hardcore pornography and was linked to the Russian Mafia. They believed the headless man found in the forest had been somehow cheating on his criminal bosses and had been butchered so as to send out a warning to others. It had been a fascinating – and chilling – introduction to the world of criminal investigation.

I'd taken part in another couple of investigations

after that, always on the same terms. I was not allowed to discuss the case publicly and the police made it clear that they would deny my involvement if anyone was to ever ask about it. And that had always suited me just fine. Indeed, I felt that was the right way to treat my work in this area. I felt that there was some work that mediums do that shouldn't be in the public eye.

I told Hilary all this back when she first suggested *Psychic Private Eyes*. There were some mediums out there who were only too happy to publicise their involvement in high-profile cases. When the little girl Madeleine McCann went missing in Portugal, a number of so-called mediums were quick to get themselves in the newspapers and on television. It made me a little ashamed of my profession, truth be told.

Hilary was a persuasive lady, however. She sat me down for a long conversation during which she argued that we would be performing a public service by investigating cases of genuine public interest that, for whatever reason, had question marks hanging over them.

Yet I'd continued to be reluctant until we received a letter from a lady called Linda Bowman.

Her daughter, Sally Anne, had been a student at the famous BRIT School and had been just starting a career as a model when she was brutally murdered, stabbed and then raped near her home in Croydon in

September 2005, just two weeks after her eighteenth birthday. No one had been apprehended for the crime and the police files were still very much open.

I learned through Hilary that Linda – and indeed her late daughter – had been fans of *6ixth Sense*. Linda had written specifically to me asking for my help.

The first exposure I had to the case had come when I was handed an envelope without any other information. It was what my mother used to do when I was a child: 'Hold this and tell me what you see.' I didn't know what to make of the vision I suddenly had in my head – it was simply a fence and some kind of factory. I could see someone observing others from behind this fence, as if waiting to strike. It was only later that I discovered that the envelope contained a photograph of Sally Anne.

Soon after this, her mother Linda asked me to visit her. I went to see her at her home in south London and was immediately aware of powerful spirit presences. Even before I'd gone into the home, I'd seen a cul-de-sac near the Bowman home. It was a recycling plant with a chain-link fence, exactly like I'd seen when I'd 'read' the envelope. It was somehow connected to the killer, I felt sure.

I warmed to the Bowman family the moment I met them. I met Linda and Sally Anne's three sisters as well as Sally Anne's boyfriend, who, for no justifiable reason, had been a suspect at one stage. In the reading I did for them, Sally Anne came through very clearly and very powerfully. It was a very moving experience in which the family were able to pass on their love to her – and vice versa. My sitting was being filmed for the television series, but was also being monitored by police. I was told later that some of the information Sally Anne passed on to me had been so accurate that one officer had snapped, 'How the f*** does he know that?'

Psychic Private Eyes drew on the talents of all three mediums involved in the show. I'd known Tony Stockwell for many years, since we'd met at that first Noah's Ark seminar in Leicester back in 1982. By contrast, the first time I met TJ – or Tracy – Higgs was when we filmed together on *Psychic Private Eyes*. We hit it off immediately. I just liked her, she was so down to earth, there was no side to her. I instantly had the feeling that she was a very gifted medium who just needed the right exposure, so I asked her to join me on future tours.

Together, the three of us assembled a mass of information that was passed on to the police and never released into the public domain. But we were able to share some of our conclusions on camera, including the facts that we saw the name 'Mark', that the killer had some connection with Australia and that Sally Anne was not the first victim of his violence.

The police investigation was a long and tortuous one, but eventually they found Sally Anne's killer. In 2007 the police arrested a man called Mark Dixie. He was tried and found guilty in February 2008 when he was sentenced to life imprisonment for murdering Sally Anne. It was revealed that he was a serial sex offender who had harassed and attacked other women.

I was personally very proud of the part that we played in Sally Anne's case, and indeed in the others we investigated as part of the *Psychic Private Eyes* series. The other case that gave me particular pride was that of another young person who had died in a violent way in London, a young man called Ricky Royle.

Ricky had been found drowned in the River Thames. The official police report into the incident had marked it down as an accidental death but his family had been convinced there was more to it than that. They suspected he had been the victim of murder. As was often the situation in *Psychic Private Eyes*, the police weren't terribly pleased that we had taken an interest in the case and at one point the producer was given a stern dressing-down by a senior policeman.

But we weren't deterred, especially when we began to get a very strong sense that Ricky's death was much more complex than the police report suggested. There were a couple of anomalies in the evidence. The police had concluded, for instance, that Ricky had gone down to the river to urinate, but a post mortem revealed his bladder was full when he died.

I visited the spot on the Thames where Ricky had

been found dead and also spoke to his parents. I was able to make a connection with Ricky in the spirit world and he angrily showed me a series of images of a black car, a group of youths and an argument. I had seen quite clearly that the gang had beaten Ricky over the head before bundling him into the boot of the car. They had then disposed of his body in the river.

The family told me that there had been CCTV footage of a black BMW in the area at the time but the police hadn't acted upon it. They didn't act on our evidence either, but in this case that was less important. My aim had been to give the family some kind of explanation for what had happened to their son and also the strength to continue fighting for justice. The fact that we achieved that made me very proud as well.

The *Psychic Private Eyes* series was a hit, becoming a favourite overseas in particular. Apparently at one point we were the number one entertainment programme in Romania! I was warned that if I ever walked down the streets in Bucharest I'd be mobbed. I was always sorely tempted to try – just to see what would happen.

Despite this success, however, I had become increasingly unhappy about my relationship with IPM. I was still under contract to the company and therefore subject to a number of contractual constraints. And there were some elements on the financial side of business that I wasn't happy with. While it had been a great experience making *6ixth Sense* with them, there was another part of me that was saying, 'I am being controlled, I am not allowed to make my own decisions.'

At one stage I turned to the spirit world and said, 'I know I asked you for "a bit more than enough" but I don't feel free to control my own life and career.' The answer I got back was simple: 'Well, do something about it.'

Unfortunately, at that point, I also received another, more familiar message. It was the voice of my great-grandmother, saying, 'Not long . . .'

Around this time we learned that Hilary was seriously ill with pancreatic cancer. Hilary was a fighter and told us all that she was determined to beat the disease. But she had a really aggressive kind of cancer and simply couldn't overcome it.

It hit me hard, especially as I was wrestling with the thought that I wanted to leave IPM. Out of respect for Hilary, I stayed with them throughout her illness. She died in 2008. I learned of her passing one morning while myself and Tracy Higgs were on tour. It was a very moving show that evening, not least because both Tracy and I felt Hilary's presence with us throughout.

Her loss devastated her husband Craig and their children, and left a huge void in her business. Craig took control of IPM afterwards and, for a while, our relationship was cordial. But I was becoming more and more convinced that I had to leave the company. By the time I played the Hammersmith Apollo as part of *The Three Mediums* tour that year I realised that I'd taken it as far as I could. That night at the London Palladium I knew that I'd reached a high point in my career and that, once more, it was time for me to turn a new page. Again Ida's words came back to me. Another group of people had served their purpose. I now had to let go.

I'd like to say that it was an amicable split but sadly it wasn't. I had sensed that leaving IPM would hit my finances hard and so it proved. The break wasn't easy and there was a long and protracted legal negotiation. It couldn't have come at a worse time for me because I was fighting another financial fire elsewhere at the time.

Over the course of my years making television pro-grammes I had invested more and more money into the Ramsbergsgarden centre. But it had become exactly what my friends had predicted – a money pit. The company that ran it had gone into receivership. I couldn't bear the idea that this wonderful Spiritualist community was going to disappear. I had invested so much emotionally – and financially. By now I had spent hundreds of thousands of pounds on it.

The ins and outs of the situation were complicated and involved lots of local laws and tax regulations. But the bottom line was that the only way for the centre to survive was for me to write off my losses and hand over ownership of the centre to the local community.

So that's what I did. Despite having invested a six-figure sum in the Ramsbergsgarden, I gifted it to Jane and Joel.

A lot of my friends and associates told me that I was a fool. What they didn't understand was that I had a very different attitude to money. Yes, I had made a lot of money from television, although not as much as some people would imagine. I wasn't a millionaire by any stretch of the imagination, although if I'd held on to every penny I'd made I would have been close.

But my view was that the spirit world had helped me make a small fortune on the understanding that it was not mine to keep. I had to use it for good. And ensuring the survival of one of the most important Spiritualist centres in Europe was – in my book anyway – a very good thing to achieve indeed. Yes, I'd once possessed a piece of paper saying that legally I owned it. But it was never mine to keep. It was always meant to be for the benefit of not just the Swedish Spiritualist community but the whole international Spiritualist community.

Of course, this had a horrendous impact on my finances. The combination of the protracted legal arguments over what I might be owed by IPM and the losses I'd run up in Sweden drove me to the brink of bankruptcy. It was a deeply worrying time in my life.

I have never been a person who worries about money a great deal. I have always worked on the principle that if I need some, it will appear.

My father had never understood this. In fact, at the height of the crisis in Sweden and at home, I had a conversation about it.

'What are you going to do when the money runs out?' he said to me, knowing that point was fast approaching.

'Dad, I will do what I always do. I will go out there and do some work and get some more money,' I replied.

But on this occasion, as bills went unpaid, and the debts racked up, I began to fear for the future. Mikey and I had a beautiful house and enjoyed a great lifestyle. But there were moments in the middle of the night when I would wake up, fearing I would lose it all. However, whenever I did, I would draw on my experience and all that the spirit world had taught me. I soon pulled myself together and did what I told my father I would do. I went out to work and tried to make some more money.

In 2010, I hired myself a brilliant new publicist, Julia Stevens, and my old friend Eden as my manager. We began planning tours not only in the UK, but in Australia and New Zealand and – new ground for me – Norway.

We headed to Tromso in August 2010. The tour, in

which we demonstrated in seven different venues – including many towns and cities that had never witnessed a live Spiritualist medium performance before – went down a storm. Such was the interest in Norway that I was approached and agreed to return to television on the Norwegian station FEM. The name of the show was *Den Andre Siden*, translated as 'The Other Side' – ironically the original name of *6ixth Sense*.

That year I also decided to broaden my knowledge of healing by studying aromatherapy and herbalism. With Mikey's help, I also began developing a range of aromatherapy oils and other products designed to aid relaxation and spirituality.

In many ways it was an echo of the days when I first turned professional. I had taken that leap of faith and the spirit world had somehow rewarded me for it. New doors were opening once more.

18 | Let It Go

Dᴜʀɪɴɢ the thirty years or so that I have been a practising medium I have seen the public's interest in my work ebb and flow. There have been periods when we have been confined to the margins of society in the Spiritualist churches and small theatres. And then there have been periods when we mediums have been celebrated as television stars, filling 3,000-seat venues. What's interesting is that the public's awareness always rises at times of tragedy, war or uncertainty in the world.

So, for instance, mediums were very much in demand during the Falklands and Gulf Wars. We saw another spike in interest in our work in the aftermath of 9/11 and, before that, witnessed an unbelievable surge when Princess Diana died back in 1997. This is something that apparently happened around both World Wars during the last century, as well as during the Wall Street Crash and the Great Depression.

So it was not really too surprising that, when the global economy went into meltdown and global recession took hold, mediumship was much in demand once more. It wasn't just that people felt insecure and uncertain about the world. As they found themselves short of money and hope, they were questioning their whole materialistic way of life.

As I returned to touring with my new company in 2011, I saw plenty of evidence of this. One message sticks in my mind. It happened in a theatre in the north of England.

The energy surrounding the man who was trying to communicate with someone in the theatre audience was a familiar one. I could sense already that he had died very suddenly of a massive heart attack.

'He is showing me the name Ingrid,' I said. 'And I am getting a strong sense of a boat or a yacht, bobbing on the water in a harbour. I'm also seeing cobwebs, which feels very strange.'

A hand went up in the audience. It was a very attractive middle-aged lady. She looked drawn and was already emotional when the microphone in the theatre reached her.

'Does that mean anything to you?' I said.

'It does,' she said. 'My name is Ingrid.'

I described the man and the sensation I was feeling of his having died suddenly in recent months. I sensed he was fifty-two years old. At this she just nodded.

The man's presence had intensified around me now and he was showing me images of letters cascading through a letter box. They were all in brown envelopes. 'I am seeing bills,' I said. 'Lots and lots of bills.'

She nodded. 'He is saying he had tried so hard to find a way out for you both,' I said. 'But he is saying there is a way out for you.'

I continued, 'Your husband is saying three words to me . . . He is saying over and over, "Let it go. Let it go."

'Do you understand what he is saying when he says that?' I asked.

'Yes, I think I do,' she said, nodding quietly.

At that point the man's energy disappeared almost as quickly as it had arrived. He had clearly passed on the message that he needed to communicate.

The lady waited to see me after the show, joining the long line of people waiting for me to sign a book or a photograph. When I saw her I asked her if she could wait until the line had thinned out so that we could talk properly. She said she didn't have far to go when she left the theatre and so agreed.

Ingrid told me that her husband, James, had been quite a successful businessman. But the recession had crippled his business and he had been left jobless with a mountain of debt. He was a good, hard-working man who had tried everything to get a new job but had been constantly frustrated. The debts were soon piling up and James's health began to suffer.

He and Ingrid didn't have any children, and had lived a very good life. They were both keen sailors and owned a small sailing dinghy which they kept on the

Yorkshire coast. 'It wasn't anything special. It wasn't a yacht or anything flash like that. But we loved it. It was called *Cobweb*, we used to jokingly call it HMS *Cobweb*,' she smiled. Over a period of eighteen months their comfortable lifestyle just disappeared. There were no more weekend breaks, no more nice dinners, and they eventually had to sell their house and rent a small apartment. It had been a humiliating fall for James, she admitted. The one thing James and Ingrid couldn't bear to part with was *Cobweb*.

'James used to say that if we gave that up then we might as well give up on life,' she said.

But James had always been overweight and drank too much, Ingrid admitted. One day, soon after he'd received another demand for a lot of money that he didn't have, he had a massive heart attack. He had been on his own at the time. Ingrid had found him dead on the landing.

That had been just under a year earlier. Since then Ingrid had been slowly rebuilding her life. She had landed a job in public relations and moved into a new apartment that she liked. She hadn't forgotten James, but she had moved on. The one link with her old life was the dinghy.

'Is that what he meant when he said, "Let it go"?' I asked her.

'I think it must be,' she said. 'I can't afford to keep paying the mooring fees and I don't ever go out in it any more. I've just kept it on because it's the last little bit of me and James's old life that is left.'

'He will live on in your heart though, won't he,' I said. 'And that's the most important thing.' I told her that I knew exactly what she was going through. She looked at me with a slightly puzzled expression. 'It's a hard time for everyone. We're all having to let it go,' I smiled. 'Even me.'

'Surely not,' she said.

I have always been very open with people about my life, perhaps a little too much so at times. But I felt comfortable sharing with her some of the experiences I'd been through. She shook her head quietly when I told her that I'd given the centre in Sweden away for nothing. I sensed she understood why I'd done it, nevertheless.

They were switching the lights off in the theatre by this time and the staff were ushering us to leave. But by now I could see a small weight lifting off Ingrid's shoulders. She wrote to me a few weeks later to tell me that she'd sold HMS *Cobweb*.

'I didn't get much money for it, but that wasn't the point. I felt so liberated by it,' she said. 'Especially knowing that it's what James wanted me to do.'

Many years ago, my first mentor, Ida, said something to me that I have always remembered. 'Colin, you will never take the easy path, it's not in your nature,' she said. 'It will be hard for you, but it will make you a better medium.'

How true that was. Ever since I began my development as a medium with her more than thirty years ago, this has been my story. Life has always had a habit of providing me with difficult, sometimes painful, experiences that I have been able to draw upon for the benefit of others. During the course of my first fifty years I have been through emotional turmoil and illness; I have had to contend with financial and career problems. I have survived each of these crises, and each time I have emerged ready to draw on the experience.

There is, of course, a reason for this. My calling, my vocation, my job is to act as a conduit, a vessel for all that the spirit world is seeking to communicate with those of us who are here on this earthly plane. The nature of those messages is always changing. But I will always remain the messenger who delivers them. So events in my life will always be preparing me to do my job.

Who knows what lies ahead? Who knows what experiences await me in the future? All I do know is that every experience I have, every moment of joy, pain and enlightenment I live through shapes me as a person, but it also makes me a better – and a happier – medium. I can't wait for the next chapter in my psychic journey . . .

Conclusion

WRITING my life story so far has been a mostly happy experience, even if it has at times been sad and painful to revisit the past. In doing so, I have had to remember when I have been hurt and when I have hurt others, loves won and loves lost, my achievements and my failures, as well as when I got things right or got them disastrously wrong! I have tried to be kind and honest in my words, even when recalling those situations out of which, in retrospect, no good was ever going to come for anyone involved!

It has occurred to me that when our soul moves on in death from this mortal life, we will all be asked to give an account of ourselves. Perhaps when we pass over, we will find ourselves in front of a huge book of empty pages in which we will be asked to write our life story and justify ourselves to eternity. Once we have filled in its pages, then and only then can we look back on those we have left behind and say: 'This is what I was, this is who I have become – and I love you, always.'

Also available from Rider:

Secrets from the Afterlife

Colin Fry

'One of TV's biggest psychic stars' *Mirror*

Colin Fry is one of our leading psychic mediums. Not only are his viewing figures huge, he also tours the country speaking to massive audiences. So many people want to see him because he's the keeper of remarkable secrets:

- When loved ones pass over, where do they go?
- How do you know if they're ok?
- Are they still aware of us?
- Can they do anything to help?
- Is there a way to keep in touch with them?

In this extraordinary book, Colin explains how understanding the spirit world has made his own life so much easier. And he also describes how many, many people ask him to connect with their loved ones who have passed over. The stories of these encounters make incredible reading. Colin reveals how the secrets from the afterlife could change your perspective forever...